OVER TO YOU

Published by
The Bournemouth & District branch of the Aircrew Association
123 Carbery Avenue, Bournemouth, Dorset BH6 3LP (Tel: 01202 434794)
© Copyright The Aircrew Association 2000 (www.aircrew.org.uk)

Printed by RPM digital (www.rpmweb.co.uk)

EDITORIAL

December 1999

Someone asked me the other day how I got involved in the job of archivist for our Branch. I certainly didn't volunteer for the job, it was impressed on me when I first joined the RAF at the tender age of 18, never, never, volunteer for anything !

I had just read the book published by the Manchester Branch of the ACA on their experiences during the war, and just happened to mention to two senior members of our committee how much I had enjoyed it and why hadn't we published something similar ourselves? I am sure they had rehearsed their reactions and were just waiting for some "innocent lamb to the slaughter" to come along. I don't know to this day how they did it but I found myself as Branch Archivist. Joking apart I'm very glad they did, it has been a great challenge and privilege to help with this publication and I hope you the readers will enjoy it as much as I have in helping to compile it.

I would like to thank firstly all the writers for their contributions and then Michèle Bevis for her French translations, Alan Mercer, Bob Janes, George Serrels, Peter Crouch and John Tulk for their typing on word processors, storing on to CD-ROMs, floppy disks, and what have you, often from the most illegible hand written sheets, and somehow, magically, coming up with legible manuscripts.

Also, the help and advice from other ACA branches, in particular Clive Watt editor of "Upside down, nothing on the clock." of the Woking Branch whose support and suggestions have proved invaluable.

The most difficult task I experienced, (apart from trying to decipher stories and escapades sometimes presented on scraps of paper), was, to overcome the typical and admirable in some ways, British reticence, "Oh, I never did much, just doing my job" and getting sufficient contributions for publication. I leave it to you the reader to judge whether these stories are "just run of the mill?" "Over to you"

Rex Hurley

In compiling this book we have used some photographs which, due to age or original recording methods used, (sometimes Box Brownies), may be of slightly lesser picture quality than usual. They have been included however to make the book as comprehensive and historically accurate as possible.

LIST AND DETAILS OF AUTHORS

Bedford Ellis - *WOP/Air/ASV/GL* -   Page 104
Served from Nov.'40 overseas, South Africa Dec.'41 to Mar.'43 with 240 Sqn. Madras on ops. and in Mar.'44 joined Flying Boat Flight of 357 and 628 Sqns. on Special Duties. Completed tour Mar.'45 then various courses Jul.'45 on Liberators. Released March '47 as a F/O

Bevis Jim - *Pilot* -   Page 201
Volunteered and joined up in Nov.42. and after 5 months waiting in Moncton Canada, went to No.3 BFTS Miami, Oklahoma for flying training. Awarded wings 1st April.'45. Flew Tiger Moths with 3 EFTS, trained as a Radar Operator and was then I/c safety equipment at Coningsby with 83 & 97 Sqns as a Parachute Packer until demobbed in `46.

Black Reg - *Pilot* -   Page 34
Joined the RAF in July '42, trained in Canada Flew Whitley's at 81 OTU then Halifax's with 1665 HCU (Airborne Support). In '45 was flying a Halifax with 644 Sqn. towing a Hamilcar on the greatest airborne offensive in history over the Rhine. Retired as a F/O

Burgess Pete - *Nav/WOP* -   Page 114
Joined Jul.'43 and awarded brevet May'44 at Cranwell. After various refresher courses was grounded in '45. Sept. was i/c Flying Control W/T section and demobbed in Mar.'47.

Burke Bill - *Navigator* -   Page 222
Joined in Sept.'42 through 'Y' entry scheme for his training. Completed tour on Lancs. Jan.'45 with 207 Sqn. and then Mosquitoes with 627 Sqn. attached to 5 Group, awarded PFF insignia. After VE Day was due to go to the Far

East as part of a Master Bomber crew but luckily the war ended and retired as a F/O in '46.

Chapman 'Chappie' *- Pilot -*   Pages 191/195

Joined up 1st Sept.'39, two days before war was declared and flew ops on Wellingtons with 57 and 75 Sqns. Became OTU instructor and later Flying Control Officer then demobbed in '46

Cook Douglas *-Pilot -*   Page 101

Joined in '48, trained at 3 FTS on Prentice and Harvard, then 203AFS on Meteors and 201AFS on Wellingtons. Flew Washingtons in 44/55 Sqn before going to Coastal Command in '52 flying Lancasters and Shackletons in 220, 120 and 224 Sqns. Exchange tour with 404 Sqn RCAF '58/60 on Neptunes and Argus. Staff tours at HQ Strike Command, MoD and HQRAF Germany. OC RAF Det Majunga '70/71, OC RAF Akrotiri '75/78. Awarded OBE '75, retired '85.

Cross Michael *- Pilot -*   Page 243

Oct`42. Gained wings. Aug `43. Flying instructor. June` 50 73 Sqn. Malta on Vampires. Dec`52. 147 Long Range Ferry Sqn. Oct`53. Seriously injured in flying accident. May `54.Returned to full flying duty. `55. E.T.P.S Farnborough. `56. Test pilot R.A.E. Farnborough. Feb`59 Retired on medical grounds as F/L Awarded AFC and Queen's commendation for valuable service in the air

Crouch Peter *- Pilot -*   Pages 176, 181, 186/190

Joined Jul.42, awarded wings in Oct '43 in Canada. Flew Whitley's/ Halifax's with 295/297 Sqn '45 to '46. '48 on Hastings with 47 Sqn. '48 to '60 in Training Command on Ansons, Prentice, Harvards, Chipmunks, Meteor/Vampires. Hunter. ('55 AFM, '57 commissioned) '60 to '62 in

Singapore. '63 to '70 with 242 OCU on the Argosy, then 215/70 Sqn in Singapore/ Cyprus. Joined Air Support Command Examining Team '70. In '72 with 46 Sqn./242 OCU on Andover C1. Retired '78 as S/L With 10.000 Hours and 50 aircraft types.

Flanagan George - B/A -   Page 124

Volunteered '40, called up '41, Canada for pilot training but had problems with the Airspeed Oxford so remustered as a B/A '42 did OTU on Whitleys at Stanton Harcourt then 2 months Coastal and Sub patrols over 'The Bay' before joining 77 Sqn at Elvington. After 2 'aborts' and 3 'ops' was shot down returning from Munchengladbac on 30 Aug.43. Two years as POW then demobbed in Nov.45

Fox Freddie - Flt Eng -   Page 71

Joined as an apprentice in '33. Flew as a mechanic on Stirling's, 1st 'Op' on Brest in '41. A founder member of the Flight Engineer aircrew trade. Did a tour with 7 Sqn. then converted to Lancs. then to 15 Sqn as a Pathfinder to complete second tour. Awarded the AFM and Polish DFC for special services. Then transferred to 242 Sqn Transport Command before joining The Kings Flight. Demobbed as a F/L

Francis 'Kiwi' - Pilot -   Page 32

Joined RNZAF in '40 , requested a posting to UK arriving Hurn in '41. Flew Spitfires and Hurricanes in Africa and Italy campaign. Flew with 32, 486, 616 (jet), 263, 226 (jet) fighter Sqns. Engaged in Vampire trials in Middle East, Far East and Sudan. Later flew 'choppers' with 194 & 275 Sqns. Awarded DFC, AFC and Bar. Retired as a F/L.

George Phil - Navigator -   Pages 232/235

Joined in '41 trained as a Navigator wholly in the UK flew Lancs with 9, 106 and 83 PFF sqns. Shot down on 11/11/'44 target Harburg (not Leonard Cheshire's fault although he was Master Bomber). Guest of the German Government in Stalag Luft III until 'liberated' by the Russians in April '45. Retired as F/L in '46.

Greaves Alan - *Pilot* - Page 170
In '43/44 trained as a pilot in S. Rhodesia and then flew Beaufighter's with 252 Sqn in Middle East. and Greece. '46/'47 with No.1 Ferry Unit Pershore ferrying various aircraft to Europe and the Far East. Retired a F/O.

Hudson David - *Navigator* - Page 17
Joined in '51 trained at No.2 ITS and No.1 Air Navigation School. Awarded Nav. Brevet in '52 and commissioned as P/O. Training flights to Malta and Libya in Wellington aircraft. Continued in Reserve and retired in '59 as a F/O.

Hurley Rex - *Pilot* - Pages 73/113
(One of the last of the many) Aug '45 after 2 years and 7 months awarded pilots wings in Texas. Having seen VE and VJ days over there, was demobbed in 46. In civvy street worked as a tech/illustrator/ artist for De Havillands, Vickers, and free lance for Flight Refuelling Normalairs, Westlands, Rolls Royce, Concorde etc.

Janes Bob - *Pilot* - Page 36
Joined Aug.'41 awarded wings May '43 in Texas. In '43 18.AFU, 1513 B.A.T. Flt, and 62 OTU. In '44/5 54 OTU. Then posted to the Far East for Jungle Courses. In '46, 89, 55 and 22 Sqns. Flew nine different types of aircraft finishing with Beaufighter and Mosquito Demobbed as a W/O in '46.

Jones Eric - *Pilot* - Page 41
Joined in '41 and awarded wings in '42. Converted to Lancs Aug.'43 with No.

49 Sqn, completing tour with twelve raids on Berlin. Awarded DFC then continued with various training and instructional courses and was demobbed in Jan. '48 as a F/ L

Jones Kenneth - *Pilot* - Page 54

Joined April.'42 and trained in '43 at EFTS and SFTS and later B & G School in S. Africa. In '44 H.C.U. flying Liberators in Palestine. Joined No.31 (S. Africa) Sqn and was awarded the Polish Cross of Valour for supply dropping. Retired '46 as a W/O.

Joy Charlie - *Nav/BA/Wop* - Page 120

Joined 1928 as engine Fitter, Volunteered for aircrew '42 and awarded brevet '43, Posted to Ceylon Xmas '43 to fly Beauforts with 22 Sqn. later converting to Beaufighters in Coastal Command. Joined SEAC at Colombo flying Beechcraft Expeditors. Demobbed Easter '46. Founder member of Bournemouth Branch ACA.

Kearns Terry - *Pilot* - Page 81

Joined the Royal New Zealand Air Force in Dec.'40. Awarded wings and arrived in UK '41. Went to Cranwell and 11 OTU to 'crew up' and completed two tours with 75(NZ) Sqn. Skipper of first crew to be awarded Path Finders Wings with 156 Sqn. Converted to Lancs in '43 and joined 617 Sqn. Later flew with BOAC from Hurn and in '49 accepted a Short Service Commission. Flew Vampires with 60 Sqn. then Canberras with 139 (Jamaica) Sqn in '56 Suez war again as a Target Marker. Retired in '63 as a S/L with DSO, DFC, DFM.

Lambourne Vic - *Wop/Ag* - Pages 157, 159, 161

Volunteered May '39. attested Jun '39. Trained at Cranwell West Freu, then 16 OTU on Hampdens at Heyford but retained as an instructor until '41 then joined 106, 209 and 12 Sqn. Early crew on Lanc.1's with 12 Sqn. Bottesford. Completed 1st tour and started 2nd tour April.43 with 12 Sqn. Did total of 56 Ops' retiring Dec.45 as S/L.

McCreith Stan. - *Pilot* -   Page 208,210

Joined in Sept.'39 & awarded wings in July.'42. Became a flying Instructor with USAAC in Alabama then flew Mosquitoes but POW in '44. In '45 with PR Development Unit Boscombe Down then ETPS, A and AEE Boscombe Down. Air Ministry Staff College 81 (PR) Sqn., RAE, AM Staff Officer then as OC Henlow before retiring as Substantive W/C in '66 with A.F.C and Bar having flown some 70 types of aircraft.

Mahon Paddy - *Pilot* -   Page 164

Joined in 1930, awarded wings in '37. Qualified on flying boats in '38 on Stranraers, Sunderland's, London's, and Catalina's. Joined 228, 10 (RAAF), & 205 Sqns until '41 when a serious accident off Gib grounded him and he returned to Technical duties. He retired as a W/C with an MBE in '67.

Mercer Alan -*Navigator* -   Page 45

Joined in '42 awarded Nav brevet in '44 .After initial, qualifying, advanced and operational training in '45 was with 1699 HCU & 214 Sqn, in B17 Fortress in 'spoof' raids followed by 570 Sqn on Stirling's. Retired as a W/O in '46.

Moss John - *Pilot* -   Page 116

Volunteered in '41 joined in '42 awarded wings in S Africa No11 OTU also in S Africa on Hurricanes. Flew via Egypt to GATU nr. Calcutta for low flying and dive bombing also on Hurricanes. Later converted to fly American L5's until VJ day. Signed on to fly jets. Retired in '54 as a F/O with AFM.

Muncer Kevin *- Pilot -*   Page 173

Joined in '39, awarded wings and posted to 502 Sqn flying Whitley's on Coastal Reconnaissance. Then a period of instructing followed by OTU on Halifax's to join 78 Sqn, converted to Lancs in '44 and joined 166 Sqn. Shot down and POW until '45 Retired in '46 as a F/O with DFC

Nicoll Alan *- Air Observer/Pilot -*   Page 20, 24, 28

Joined in '39 as Air Observer & went to 44 Sqn on Hampdens flying on first 'op' of the war Completed 37 sorties and became Specialist Nav. Trained as a pilot in '44 and flew Sunderland's in `46, rejoined in `50 and held various posts and retired in '75 as a S/ L after 33 years.

Plunkit Bill *- Navigator -*   Page 130

Flew with No.77 Sqn on Halifax's. Shot down on a raid to Berlin on 23rd Aug.'43. POW with Geo. Flannagan and demobbed late '45.

Pocock Slim *- Navigator -*   Page 215

Joined as an apprentice in '45. Commissioned and obtained Nav. brevet in '51 Became F/C in '52 then with 100, 97, & 83 Sqns until '59. Was with 2nd Op crew to qualify on Vulcans. '59/60 Tech. author, 60/62 Radar Inst. on Vulcan OCU. From '63 weapons training on 10 plus 66, & 83 Sqns Low level strike, fighter control, early warning and communications. Senior Ops Officer Northolt and demobbed as a F/L.after 38 years.

Rowland Mostyn *-Observer -*   Page 77

Volunteered and Joined in Jul. '41 Awarded brevet in May.'42 Flew in Whitleys and baled out in Jun.'42 and ditched in Irish Sea three months later. Converted to Lancaster's with 101 Sqn and finished tour in '43. Awarded DFM. and demobbed in Jan '46 as F/O.

Serrels George *-Pilot -* Page 217, 220

Volunteered and Joined `40. Trained in S Rhodesia, awarded wings in `42. 28 O.T.U. at Wymeswold, Converted to Halifax's at 1667 Con Unit, then Lancaster's at No1 LFS .Hemswell Completed tour of Ops with 166 Sqn. `45 posted to 355 MU Salawas India. `46 298 Sqn Burma. `47 TFU Defford. Retired `48 as F/L having flown 22 aircraft types

Sickelmore Stan *- Pilot -* Page 203

Volunteered in '41, trained as a pilot in America and Canada. Joined 138 Sqn on Spec. Duties in '44 on Stirling's and converted to Lancs in '45. Left RAF in '47 to fly as civil airline pilot until '75.

Skinner Ernest *- Navigator/BA -* Page 111

Joined in '41 and awarded Nav/BA brevet in '42. Flew Baltimores in '43/'44 with 75 OTU and 69 Sqn in Italy. Converted to B25/ Mitchell's with No.2 GSU and 226 Sqn then Mosquitoes with 128 Sqn. Competed a tour of 'Ops' on B25 Mitchell's and then to BAFO Comm. Wing flying Avro X1X's in '46 Retired as a F/O.

Smeaton Joe *- WOP/AG -* Page 86

Joined in '40 and awarded WOP half wing in '41 First Op to Bremen on Hampden and in '42 with 49 Sqn to complete first tour. Volunteered for 2nd tour and flew with 90 Sqn in '43 completing 2nd tour (25 ops) in '45 on Lancs Awarded DFC and demobbed as a W/O.

Smith Bernard *- Navigator/BA -* Page 154

Joined in '43 and awarded Nav/BA brevet in '44 in Canada having trained at US Naval Base Michigan, 31 B & G School Ontario and No.2 School of Navigation Canada. In '45 at No.4 (O) AFU and in '46 with No1 Parachute Training School and then Tangmere. Demobbed in '47.

Spencer-Fleet Ron - *Flt Eng.* - Page 138

Volunteered and joined up in '42 and awarded Flight Engineers brevet in '43. Trained at 1651 HCU then crewed up and joined 620 Sqn. Shot down over Germany 30/31 of july.'43 and was POW until April '45. Released in January '47 as a W/O

Trott Ken - *Pilot* - Page 94, 96, 98

Volunteered and called up in Sept '41 awarded wings in Oct '42. Flew Hurricanes then Typhoons doing about 80 sorties until made POW in '44. Released as a F/L and became Air Traffic Control Officer at Tangmere in '46.

Tulk John - *Pilot* - Page 238

Joined as Cadet, Mar.'48, among first direct entry a/c. Awarded wings 6 FTS Sep.'49, Trained again at RAF College. Joined 10 Sqn. (2nd Canberra sqn) '52. Qualified QFI '54 Served with 101 Sqn (2nd Vulcan sqn) '57-'60. On loan to Rolls Royce for engine tests using Vulcan test-bed. '60-'63 RAF Handling Sqn Boscombe Down. Back injury led to ground job at 1 S of TT Three years later instructing at Manby but invalided out in '69. due to further back injury as a F/L

Venning Doug - *F/L Engineer* - Page 63, 66, 69

Enrolled Jan. '43 and became F/Eng/F2E attaining brevet July .'44. Flew with 620 Sqn on Stirling's on SOE, Airborne Ops and Strategic Bombing. Converted to Halifax V11's in '45 with Airborne Brigade and Horsa Glider operations. M.E. and Met flights etc for 2 years and 7 months with same skipper and demobbed in Jul.'47.

Williams Tom - *WOP/Air Gunner* - Page 14

Enrolled 'Jun.41, attended No3 Radio School, became WOP/AG in Apl.'42. Torpedo and T Unit on Beauforts then to Malta and Cairo to join 39 /47 Sqns.

In '43, British Airways, Cairo to Jo'burg on Sunderland's, then with 47 Sqn, 458 Sqn on Wellingtons and until Jun.44 on Hudson's and Venturas. In 45/'46 on Baltimore's and Liberator's retiring as a F/O.

Apologies to the authors who served 30 or 40 years (or more) and their whole career had to be condensed to just 4 or 5 lines.

FAMOUS LAST WORDS

"It's only friendly fire"
"Is this the ejector butt...?"
"Only an idiot would mistake that Blenheim for a JU88"
The Mayor of Hiroshima, "What the....was that"
The Mayor of Dresden, "Who let that ruddy bull in?"
The Kommandant of the Mona Dam, "Vot damn swinehun
is veeing over my vall?"

FAMOUS LAST WORDS OF THE KAMIKAZEE PILOT

"Here we go, here we go, here we go."
"I wonder what's for supper tonight?"
"I could have sworn it was an American carrier."
"XXXX this for a job."
"I've just got time for a quick XXXX."
"What's that smell?"
"Dam it, missed again."
"I must change that ruddy wallpaper when I get back."
TÆLIHÓU (Translated) "TALLY HO"

Take your pick

NOT IN THE LOG BOOK

By Tom Williams

The events to which I refer occurred in the early summer of 1941. We, Wop./A.G's. having completed our initial square bashing and morse in the Blackpool tram sheds, were posted to Yatesbury wireless school in Wiltshire, there the technical instructors were good and the camp conditions and routines, run by a sadistic and unhappy bunch of discipline Sergeants and corporals, were appalling. My memories of Yatesbury were of poor sanitation, rushed meals, universal jankers and an incredible amount of illness and disease. The hospital was full with serious and very seriously ill inmates and a number of huts were housing quarantine patients. After reporting sick twice, medicine and duty, I was eventually put in a quarantine with German Measles, then transferred to hospital with Scarlet Fever. However, we mostly survived and ended our purgatory as qualified wireless operators and were eagerly awaiting posting to an Air Gunnery School, but, oh no, we were informed that there was a bottle neck in the system and that we would all be posted to RAF stations on general duties.

Disappointed but still happy to leave the mud of Yatesbury, we went our various ways. I went to Filton near Bristol, home of Blenheim, Beaufort, and Beaufighter, but my general duties were cleaning and polishing the Senior NCO's quarters, or walking the drome with sack and sticker picking up any litter. It was while on this exciting duty that I was approached by the Senior Warrant Officer. He addressed me by name and said "You have a motor cycle Williams!", "yes Sir" said I. "Right" he said "I have a job for you, we will give you a full tank of petrol, service for the use of, you will report to Portreath in Cornwall". The West country was not overloaded with vehicles in those days, I made good time with a relatively short break for a broken chain link, repaired by an R.A.C. motor cyclist fortunately passing by. At Portreath after accommodation and a meal I was informed that they had a Blenheim not currently being made use of. They had a pilot under a cloud for dropping an expensive machine in the Severn , a navigator 'on rest', having been rescued from the channel after an Op, a rigger and a fitter and now with me, they had a Wop/AG. I did modestly point out that, whilst I was a newly appointed Wop/AG, I had not even seen a machine gun, so they showed me one, an old WW1 which would certainly not fit into a turret!. They then informed me that the specific Blenheim had no wireless transmitter/receiver 1082/1083, but they would obtain same and I could fit it up. When I pointed out that I was a sprog Wop. not a wireless mechanic I was informed that there was another Blenheim on the drome, about a mile away. I could connect up by following the wiring from one to another. After some days and many miles, I eventually completed the job and to my amazement actually got through to ground control. In the meantime I had of course got to know the Pilot, navigator (Sergeants), rigger and fitter and I as a lowly AC2 had been welcomed to the fold which included pints of mild and bitter at the Pub in Redruth.

We were ready to go, we took off, my very first experience of flight and it seemed we were detailed to an area outside Falmouth harbour, I don't think we ever saw anything and the only other duty our pilot carried out was to beat up his girl friends house. The only other incident I can remember was when we returned on one engine, I cannot remember how long this went on but I was happier there than at Filton and certainly Yatesbury. Then came a signal for me to report to Prestwick for a course that meant nothing. I feared once again being diverted from aircrew, but no, Prestwick was a course in air to surface vessel radar, all very hush hush but that's another story. I don't know whether these Blenheim trips could be considered Op's, pretty innocuous, but having no log book, unrecorded.

BROMIDE STORY

Nameless

Overheard at a certain table at the Bournemouth Branch ACA at the Flying Club, Hurn Airport. The discussion had lightly dwelt on the "cocktail of injections" that the troops had been given during the desert war, the side effects and the aftermath.

There was silence for a while when someone who shall remain nameless mentioned that whilst on fatigue duties in the first week of his RAF service at Aircrew Reception Centre, London, saw sackfuls of Bromide in the kitchens waiting to go into the tea, this was supposed to have, shall we say, a calming effect on young virile cadets. Someone said it would appear to have had the opposite effect in 1942 but seemed to have a delayed action and 50 odd years later it was just beginning to work. The whole table nodded thoughtfully as they lapsed into a contemplative and wistful silence! Eventually the subject got round to `VIAGRA` and someone said " I couldn't care less about the possible side effects in 20-30 years time, at least it stops me rolling out of bed and spending the night on the floor!

NATIONAL SERVICE

By David Hudson

David Hudson was born in Derbyshire in 1932 and started his career with the Westminster Bank in 1959. In July 1951 he received a Postal Order for 4 shillings (his first days pay) and reported to the Recruitment Office in Padgate. His aircrew Selection Board sat in Hornchurch and having been accepted he was posted first to Driffield and then to Digby, in Lincolnshire, for grading on Tiger Moths, However he never flew in one. In September 1951 he was posted to No.2 I.T.S. at Kirton-in-Lindsey, Humberside and three months later started flying at No.1 Basic Air Navigation School at Hullavington, Wiltshire. Approximately 330 flying hours and one year later he became the proud owner of a Navigator's brevet and had his commission confirmed.

During that training, initially, he flew in Ansons and Valettas graduating after three months to Advanced Training on Wellingtons. Day flying was essentially Continental trips and night flying was always confined to Great Britain, usually 1a.m. take off, and invariably was diverted to Shawbury due to fog at base. As part of the course he took a Wellington to Malta (Luqa) for a long week end and later a Valetta to Libya (Castle Benito), By then Wellingtons were 'clapped out', they were banned from leaving the U.K. (Hercules XV1 engines). On these trips he landed at Istres, in SE France for refuelling, meteorological forecast and breakfast.

After Hullavington, he did not fly again, his last six months were spent in the Search and Rescue Co-ordination Centre HQ18 Group, at Pitreavie Castle in Fife. At the end of his two years he was earning £4 per day. He returned to the Bank on approximately half pay and still had to find his board and lodging!.

Following his National Service he returned for two weeks each year for a period of six years on the Reserve, reporting to HQ Coastal Command, Northwood where he was normally involved with the annual NATO exercise, On two occasions flew down to ST. Mawgan, (good beaches!), flying down with the Communications Flight from Bovingdon either by Anson or Chipmunk, (not much room in the latter for kit). Promotion was very rapid on the Reserve, eventually making Flight Lieutenant.

Wellington

He has now destroyed the Railway Warrant enabling him to report to Northwood in a National Emergency, but cannot understand why he was not summoned for the Falklands War, which was run from Northwood. He considers himself to have been extremely fortunate in life, and very much appreciated the opportunity that National Service gave him to fly with the RAF air crews. Having been run down after WW2, and the Korean War having started in 1950 gave the opportunity for a few National Servicemen to train as pilots and navigators. On returning to the Bank, he served around Derbyshire, West Midlands, Head Office in London, Wiltshire, Oxfordshire (three years at the Bank's Staff Collage as Tutor in Behavioural Sciences), Devon, Dorset and Hampshire, retiring early at his request after 42 years and 8 months as a banker.

He now lives, with his wife Pat, in Lyndhurst and is a keen member of both the Bournemouth and District and Southampton branches of the Aircrew Association. Finally, David Hudson states, Quote "I would like to have served in World War2, but would wish to have survived".

"NO..... BUT I KNOW A MAN WHO DOES."

POEM

A PRU Pilot called Evans
Was way way up in the heavens
Fell out of his Spit
Said "Oh, what a twit"
So high he hasn't got down yet

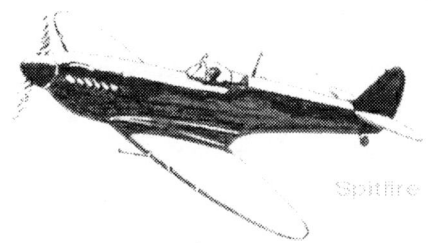

THE FIRST DAY OF WORLD WAR 2

By A. Nicoll

There cannot now be many who served as aircrew before World War 2, and even less are those who took part in an operational sortie on the first day. Now in my 80th year I was one of the lucky survivors, but memories of 3rd September 1939 and events of 60 years ago might be of interest.

In 1938 I was 18 years old with my first job as a junior in the London office of a property company. An advertisement for recruits to train as Direct Entry Air Observers with immediate promotion to Sergeant caught my eye. With domestic circumstances requiring that I should stand on my own two feet, I was prompted to apply. An interview and medical followed and I was accepted.

My initial instructions were to present myself in civilian clothes at No. 7 Elementary & Reserve Flying Training School at Desford Aerodrome near Leicester on 6th February 1939 to commence navigation training. On arrival I found I was one of 50 students. Accommodation was in a small bungalow and there was a newly built Mess: it was a promising start. No one was in uniform as the establishment was run by a civilian firm under contract.

The course lasted 12 weeks and included ground lectures and air exercises in Avro Anson aircraft. I passed out third at the end of April with 36 hours flying experience. 40 of us travelled south to RAF Uxbridge, 10 having failed to make the grade for academic reasons or air sickness.

We spent two hectic weeks at Uxbridge. We received our uniform and other items of kit (I still have my shoe brushes) did PT, drill, had lectures on

Service etiquette and we polished buttons and boots. At the end of the second week we marched out of the gates in uniform and took the Northbound train from Kings Cross. Our destination was No. 2 Air Observers School at RAF Acklington, for armament training.

Acklington was a small hutted camp with a grass airfield to the North of Newcastle. Range facilities were at nearby Druridge Bay, a long sandy beach on the Northumberland coast. There were bombing targets off shore and approved areas for air gunnery. The aircraft were Hawker Hinds for bombing and gunnery plus twin engined Overstrands for bombing. The Overstrands were monstrous biplanes, descendants of WW1 heavy bombers and real museum pieces. We also had the use of Fairey Seals, a single engine biplane. It had an open rear cockpit about the size of a bath so that two student could fly together on air firing exercises.

The course comprised three weeks bombing with lectures on the bomb sight and air practices. The gunnery course involved sighting theory and stripping and reassembling the two machine guns in common use at that time. These were the .303 Browning and the Vickers 'K' gun, the latter being used for air firing when we fired at ground targets or towed drogues .

I passed out as an Acting Sergeant Air Observer on the 26th June 1939. Nearly all of us were destined for newly formed Hampden squadrons at Lincolnshire bases of Waddington, Scampton and Hemswell, there being two squadrons at each base.

My posting to No. 44 squadron at Waddington where we began familiarisation with the new aircraft. This included Group and Command exercises. On the 18th July I was detailed to fly on a formation practice. We climbed into cloud where the pilot of one aircraft lost control. The aircraft crashed into the ground and all four occupants were killed, one a course colleague. A sharp reminder that even in peace time flying could be hazardous. The 3rd September 1939 was a Sunday and the International situation had long been tense. I was in the Sergeants Mess Ante Room reading the newspapers after breakfast. The wireless was switched on and we heard Mr Chamberlain, the Prime Minister, make the solemn announcement that we were 'at war with Germany'.

Soon after this dramatic news we were told to assemble after lunch in the Operations Room. The outcome of an address by the Station Commander was that 9 Hampdens from 44 Squadron were to carry out a low level attack that evening as part of a joint force with 9 aircraft from Scampton. The targets were warships at Wilhelmshaven. Our force was to be led by our much respected C.O. Wing Commander John Boothman. He had won the Schneider Trophy for Britain.

I was detailed as one of the navigators. I was 19 years old, with a total of 86 hours flying experience, 6 being at night. Strangely, I cannot remember any particular emotion either feeling apprehensive or frightened. One had to go with the tide so I resigned myself to my fate with the naive thought that it will 'Never happen to me'.

As to the raid itself, a paragraph in the 'The Hampden File', an excellent book by Harry Moyle who was a student with me, expresses things perfectly. I quote; "Indecision about the type of bomb to be used in the attack had caused delays in the time of take-off, and it was after 1800 hours before the two separate formations had become airborne. Neither had reached the target area before darkness descended, so no aircraft was able to make an attack. Most of the eighteen pilots involved had never flown a Hampden at night before, none had actually taken off with a full load, so that even though the operation achieved no military success, and the return flight across the North Sea was an undignified 'follow my leader' straggle, with navigation lights switched on, and it is a tribute to the pilots that all of the aircraft were safely back on the ground at their bases by around midnight". After landing we returned to the crew room where everyone indulged in some whisky, a practice which was never repeated!.

Neither disaster nor success I'm afraid, but on the positive side lessons were learned. Much more training was obviously required. It was 21st December 1939 before raid No, 2 and due to a hard winter with much deep snow on the grass airfields it was June 1940 before I was involved in operations on a nightly basis.

I have no record that youthful innocence and naivety proved correct. Fate dealt kindly with me as I subsequently survived a full tour before posting.

THE LAST RAF AIRCRAFT TO VISIT THE POOL OF LONDON

By Alan Nicoll

For several years after World War 2 as part of the commemoration of the RAF's great victory in the Battle of Britain, it was the custom to display an aircraft in London. This occurred in the week-long celebrations each September when a Sunderland flying boat was required to alight on the Thames and moor up in the Pool of London.

The sortie was undertaken by an aircraft from RAF Pembroke Dock, where the last two operational squadrons of flying boats (Nos.201 and 230) were based. In 1956 it was announced that it would be the last year as in 1957 the squadrons would be disbanded and the station closed. All the remaining flying boats would be sent to the Far East and they would be withdrawn in 1958.

In 1956 I was one of five captains on 201 Squadron whose turn it was to provide the aircraft. A lottery was held, and my good fortune was to be selected for the sortie.

The aircraft had to be a worthy representative. Sunderland Mk,5, DP 198 was selected. It was built in wartime as a Mk 3 with Bristol Pegasus engines and served with No.423 Canadian Squadron in W.W 2. Later it was updated to Mk.5 standard with a new radar fit and replacement engines, the more powerful Pratt and Whitney Twin Wasps. It was sent to the Far East and was involved in the Korean war. Afterwards, it was returned to the UK and was allocated to 201 Squadron.

The aircraft was entrusted to the O.C. Technical Wing to provide it in pristine condition. Thoroughly cleaned internally, it was launched after overhaul freshly painted in the current livery of white with a large squadron number on both sides of the hull, with roundels and the aircraft letter "A". Although it was 14 years old I was proud to have an aircraft in "show room condition".

More mundane preparations in London involved the positioning of marine craft. A powered dinghy was required to convey crew and passengers to and from the jetty, and a sea-plane tender, radio equipped, to act as a taxying escort and for local contact with the aircraft. An aircraft rubber mooring buoy had also to be laid.

Other preparations included liaison with the Port of London Authority (A "Notice to Mariners" was issued), with the London Traffic Control (Routing, Radio Frequencies and Flight Plan) and the domestic arrangements. Accommodation was provided by the military at the Tower of London. The past experience of previous Captains was certainly helpful to me.

My brief was to make courtesy calls during our stay on the Lord Mayor of London, the Chairman of the Port of London Authority, and the Governor of the Tower. We were to offer hospitality in return, and were allowed to invite personal guests aboard though the aircraft was not open to the general public. The bomb room loaded with supplies of Sherry and Beer, tea, coffee and some light snacks. The Officers Mess lent us glassware and crockery along with a table cloth and extra cushions in the Ward room.

On the 11th September 1956 we took off with myself as Captain, 11 crew and 5 passengers (a servicing party). The flight was quite uneventful with the alighting made down stream as the distance between Tower and London bridges (The Pool of London) is too short for touchdown. We had to alight at low tide as there would be no movement of larger vessels. Slack water is an advantage when mooring up but low tide means a minimum water depth, and there are mud banks for the unwary.

Below Tower Bridge there is a NW-SE reach followed by a pronounced U bend by Canary Wharf. The wind was from the West so I alighted on a westerly heading along the bottom of the U. It was of somewhat restricted length and I had to be mindful of some buildings, cranes and chimneys on the south bank. Safely down with the seaplane tender in company we taxied towards Tower Bridge, with the RAF ensign flying from the mast we erected on the hull roof. Approaching the bridge the arms of the roadway were raised for a more formal arrival, though clearance might have actually allowed us underneath. Next, the tricky bit...an 'S' turn in a confined space was necessary to make an approach to the buoy. It was positioned alongside the Traitor's Gate and fairly close to the promenade. And there were hundreds of people lining the bank to watch!. The Bowman did their stuff, and with some relief I cut the engines as they indicated we were secured.

Our stay was a very enjoyable one - our accommodation in the Tower involved being privy to the daily password to gain entrance after public hours. We had a guided tour of the Armouries and a visit to the Jewel House for a leisurely viewing in advance of its opening to the general public.

I duly presented myself to the Lord Mayor for a sherry at the Mansion House on the first day, and later completed the other required calls. We were able to entertain a number of guests. My secondary schooling had been at Coopers' Company's School when it was at Bow. I rang the Headmaster who accepted an invitation to visit on behalf of two pupils and a master. When they arrived the master remembered me from my school days in 1932-1937.

The visit finished on 17th September. This time a North West wind was blowing so the take off was directly up the NW reach which was no problem for a lightly laden aircraft. An uneventful return to Pembroke Dock followed.

We all have an abiding memory of an unusual occasion. Our souvenirs include a splendid picture of the aircraft taxying through Tower Bridge taken by the official Air Force photographer. This was matched by an excellent photo taken by one of my Signallers with the aircraft's heavy hand held camera. It was from the marine tender and shows the aircraft at moorings with the White Tower in the background and a pleasing cloud formation overhead. It has been good enough to appear in books about the Sunderland.

As a post script, the aircraft was again deployed to the Far East where on posting I flew it many times. It was one of the last two survivors of the fleet before scrapping.

A TRAGEDY OF FRIENDLY FIRE

By Sqn Ldr Alan Nicoll RAF Retd

The late Harry Moyle, who died in February 1991, was a member of the Bournemouth branch of the ACA. Had he lived, he would certainly have had a contribution to make to the Archives. As a tribute to his memory I submit this account, as I was concerned in a minor way in the incident in which he was involved.

I first met Harry Moyle on 6 Feb 1939 when we reported for training as Direct Entry Air Observers at RAF Desford, His service number immediately preceded my own. Together we completed the twelve-week Navigation Course, then followed with 6 weeks armament training at RAP Acklington. Together we were posted on 24 Jun 1939 to 44 Squadron at RAF Waddington that had just been re-equipped with the Handley Page Hampden bomber. On the outbreak of war we were immediately involved in operations.

On 21 Dec 1939 a combined force of 24 Hampdens from Waddington and Scampton was ordered to locate and bomb the pocket battleship Deutschland reported to be in the vicinity of the Norwegian coast. Harry and I were detailed as crew members; I navigated one aircraft, while he flew as the lower rear gunner in another, L 4089. I recorded my take-off time as 07.50 The formation assembled over Lincoln and we set out across the North Sea. It was thought that the ships would attempt a passage close in to neutral Norway. Spread out in line abreast we carried out a search northwards along the Norwegian coast. The weather deteriorated, low cloud forced us down at times to 500 feet, and in poor visibility with frequent rain and sleet showers we degenerated into a loose gaggle. At the prudent limit of endurance the

Hampdens had not had a sighting of any naval vessel so the formation turned Westward with the intention of landing at Lossieimouth, as planned, to shorten the return journey. In worsening conditions the squadrons became separated, Scampton aircraft making a landfall on the Northumberland coast where most landed at Acklington. One crashed on the approach due to fuel shortage killing two of the crew

The Waddington Hampdens altered course slightly northwards. When land was sighted we found ourselves to be further south than calculated, and unexpectedly approaching the Firth of Forth. The shore radar stations and Hurricanes of 72 Squadron from RAF Drem intercepted the straggling formation and informed their controller. 602 Squadron (City of Glasgow) Auxiliary squadron was at Drem flying Spitfires and they too were scrambled. Two of their pilots misidentified the Hampdens as German Dorniers, and attacking them they shot down L 4089. The aircraft ditched off North Berwick and sank within 15 seconds, the Observer/Rear Gunner (Harry Moyle) going down with the aircraft before he managed to free himself and surface. The four members of the crew were kept afloat by their Mae Wests until a fishing boat arrived and picked them up. A third Spitfire attacked L 4090 killing the Wop/AG and injuring the observer who lost one eye. This aircraft also ditched and in neither case did the dinghies function properly, We landed at RAF Drem without incident.

In the ensuing court of inquiry many problems were identified. The primary ones were a failure of communications between the Commands, poor aircraft recognition by the fighters, and technical problems with aircraft dinghies.

My own part as a Navigator was minimal, but I think a word of praise is due to the pilots. Our flight time was 7 hours 40 minutes. Due to the narrow cockpit of the Hampden it is not normally possible to leave the pilot's seat.

Thus he was strapped in for around eight hours, from dawn to dusk, as it was the shortest day of the year. He was manually flying the aircraft in loose formation in turbulent weather conditions, poorly placed if attacked by the enemy and later with positional and fuel consumption worries; it was only dogged determination which enabled us to complete the flight. The outcome of the operation was a tally of 3 aircraft lost, 3 aircrew killed and 4 wounded without ever being in contact with the enemy. Battles are not won by hard luck stories but Fate dealt us a hard blow and the poor return for our efforts cannot be attributed to the bomber aircrew.

Harry Moyle had a further traumatic flight in very bad weather in August 1940. The physical illness that resulted caused his withdrawal from flying duties. It was about 40 years before we met again as members of the ACA, and I discovered that in retirement we lived less than 10 miles apart. He developed an interest in aeronautical history and over many years with a prodigious amount of research he wrote what must be regarded as the definitive work on Hampden operations. It was published in 1989 entitled "The Hampden File" in the Air Britain series and is a worthy memorial to him.

There is an unusual postscript to include. Sgt Reid was the navigator of the other aircraft shot down, L 4090. He had flown as an airline pilot with the original British Airways on Lockheed 14 aircraft before the war. Granted 'recovery' leave after his ditching he went to London and met up with his former Captain. He too had transferred to the RAF and was flying Hudsons in a newly formed Photo Development Unit. At the Captain's suggestion Sgt Reid applied to join this squadron, and his request was granted. On 3 Mar 1940 they were flying together on a routine flight taking photos of RAF airfields so that the effectiveness of the camouflage could be assessed. They were at 7000 feet over Gravesend in perfect weather when three Hurricanes attacked the Hudson causing it to crash in flames. Tony Reid was the only one to escape by parachute being badly burned. He recovered after several months in hospital at a burns unit. Within 4 months he had been shot down twice by our own forces and had qualified for the goldfish club, the caterpillar club, and the guinea pig club. In the same period he was awarded the DFM for a daylight photographic reconnaissance flight to Kiel.

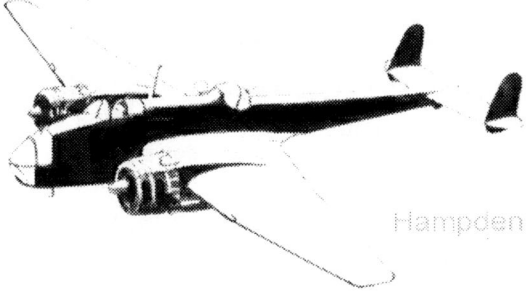

I suspect that his opinion of the standard of aircraft recognition in Fighter Command at that time would be unprintable.

A HOT PILOT
George `Kiwi` Frances

By Rex Hurley

Fifty years ago `Kiwi` was testing the Vampire Jet fighter under tropical and desert conditions where the cockpit temperature would some-times be 170 degrees, so, pilots operating in the recent Gulf war have a lot to thank him for.

`Kiwi` joined the New Zealand Air Force at the outbreak of war and flew Spitfires and Hurricanes in the N. African and Italian campaigns. He lived for flying and stayed in after the war flying Meteors and Vampires, testing the aircraft, pilots and ground crews under extreme conditions. He later converted to helicopters and was in the 1st helicopter squad at Kuala Lumpur operating against the Communists in the Malayan jungle. He often didn't go back to base every night but landed at friends rubber plantations. "I sometimes got into hot water but it was hot anyway!". He was awarded the

AFC in 1945 and a bar added in 1949. He also won the DFC for his operations in Malaya, the first pilot to be decorated on piston, jet and

helicopters and became an honorary member of the Siamese Air Force.

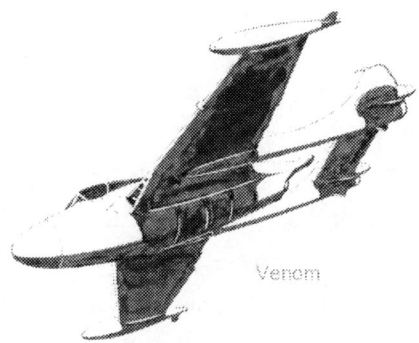

His last posting was to RAF Uxbridge operating the fully computerised Air Defence of G. B. System at West Drayton, and came out in 1974 after 34 years.

Now eighty two and a grandfather of two he is enjoying his well earned retirement playing hot music, piano, banjolele and percussion instruments with local bands.

OPERATION 'VARSITY'

By Reg Black.

The largest airborne offensive in history. During the autumn of 1944, the Allied Armies had advanced steadily towards Germany, but hopes of a Rhine Crossing before the spring of 1945 were dashed by the German counter attack in the Ardennes in December 1944. By February 1945 plans were completed for the First Allied Airborne Army to operate in support of the central group of Armies for the crossing of the Rhine. Unlike operation 'Market' (Arnhem) which was such a disaster, the Airborne Forces were to be ancillary to the main force after they had launched their ground assault.

The area of Emmerich-Wessel was chosen as being the most suitable for airborne landings. The British 6th Airborne Division was tasked to secure the northern part of the assault area, to seize high ground east of Bergen and bridges over the Issel river, to capture the town of Hamminkeln, to protect the northern flank of the U.S.16th airborne corps and the U.S.17th airborne division.

The British 6th airborne division was to be lifted by 38 and 48 groups and 52 wing of the U.S.9th Troop Carrier Command. 38 group had 10 squadrons of 30 aircraft plus 14 from the operational training unit. 46 group had 4 squadrons of 24 Dakotas and 2 squadrons of 12 aircraft, a total of 194 Stirlings, 120 Halifaxs and 120 Dakotas, they towed 386 Horsa gliders and 48 Hamilcar gliders. The two Tarrant Rushton squadrons 298 and 644 being the only ones to tow Hamilcars. Shortage of aircrews made it necessary to use Tour expired aircrew and 20 Stirlings from the Operational refresher training unit.

After months of softening up by bombers and fighter bombers, on the 24th March the greatest airborne offensive in history was launched in the early morning. 439 Tug/Glider combinations being launched in one hour to join the stream of 1500 aircraft and 1300 gliders on their way to the Rhine. The weather was perfect with a huge fighter umbrella the enemy fighter opposition was negligible and no flak was encountered until we reached the L.Z. (Landing Zone).

The RAF losses were very light, 4 aircraft shot down and 32 damaged. The U.S. aircraft lost 46 with 348 damaged. The difference was probably because the RAF flew at 2500ft while the U.S. flew at only 1000ft. General Eisehower said "The great operation of forcing the lower Rhine proved successful to the fullest extent of my desire".

Personal note - I flew a Halifax towing a Hamilcar glider which contained a bulldozer with 4 army lads and the two glider pilots. The aircraft suffered damage to the hydraulic system so once the flaps and undercarriage were lowered by the emergency system it was impossible to raise them again making an overshoot impossible. Fortunately all crew members were unhurt.

SO YOU WANT TO BE A NIGHT FIGHTER PILOT

By Bob Janes

Is it possible the London Blitz was responsible for my four years training to become a qualified night fighter pilot?.

War was declared when I was aged seventeen and working in Fleet Street. During nights of fire watching, to see the City burning behind the silhouette of St. Pauls, knowing little could be done in defence, apart from the gun barrage, and with families spending nights in underground stations and shelters made its mark.

So in 1941, evading a very large Guardsman who insisted I was right chap to join the Guards, I made it into the RAF recruitment office in Acton. Then having survived the Selection and medical boards at Oxford, I was sent home on six months deferred service.

February 1942 saw me at A.C.R.C. then I.T.W. at Paignton, followed in June by Grading School at Shellingford in Oxfordshire, low and behold there was an aeroplane. Just twelve hours flying instruction, including a solo in eight hours, would now decide if I were a suitable candidate for pilot training. Later at Heaton Park this was confirmed.

Some weeks were spent there and came the day when we were told we would be going to America. How?. After an all night train journey, at five o'clock one morning, on a jetty in Gourock, we embarked on board a ship which had an enormous hole in the sharp end, big enough to get two double Decker buses through. This to a land lubber like me, seemed a bit odd. We were told by the crew they had cut a cruiser in half on the way in. You began to wonder how the Captain had fared on his first solo, but as they allowed him out with the "Queen Mary", it must be fairly safe. In the event he got us safely to Boston in the U.S.A., the only other dry dock in the world apart from Southampton, that would take the Q.M.. So there we were one evening, bands playing, everywhere lights ablaze, which after the blackout seemed incredible. We stayed awake that night in a train, looking at the flashing lights in the towns we were passing through. Destination Moncton. Two weeks later I discovered that I was going to Terrell, Texas, which meant another three days in a train.

Time spent at No.1 B.F.T.S. in Texas is another story. Our course, No.13, included six American cadets, primarily to study our navigation. They were destined to fly Dakota's from India over the Hump into China, with no Master Navigator to lead.

Since then I have remained in contact with two in particular and they both say "thank goodness for British navigation it saved my life". The big day, Wings Parade, was 17th May 1943. Home again, on the Louis Pasteur to Liverpool. At Harrogate we were interviewed on our preference for which type of aircraft we wished to fly, what for I never found out, as thirty of us were posted to 18 (P.A.F.U. Snitterfield for conversion to twins (Oxfords).

Thirty pilots all destined for Heavy Conversion Units. A BAT course at Bramcote, (above average), then back to Snitterfield to finish with a High Average rating overall. However here the influence of the Blitz surfaced, it prompted me to request to fly night fighters. Somehow the C.O., an ex night fighter pilot, I learned later, fixed it. So while 29 went to heavies, I went to 62 O.T.U. Ouston (Newcastle) highly elated, but came back to earth when all this O.T.U. had was Ansons equipped with Mark 4 radar. When I said I was expecting Beaufighters or Mosquitos, the answer was" with two hundred and fifty hours flying you must be joking".

So what do we do here?. You are a staff pilot flying with a tour expired radar operator and two students. The Ansons operate in pairs and while the students are taught radar interceptions, you will be learning true and tried attack patterns as used by the radar instructor and his pilot. In the event it proved a very valuable experience. Previously both the tour expired pilot and his radar operator had done this job in their rest period.

Where to now - Oct.1944 12(P) A.F.U. Grantham a weeks Navigation/Beam approach brush up on Oxfords. Then on to Blenheims V's. Although we had lost pilots, some killed along the way, now I was to see, while waiting to take off, within yards of me two pilots burn to death in a crashing Blenheim, attempting to go round again. Within ten minutes I was cleared to take off on another runway. After another week of concentrated night flying I was posted to 54 O.T.U. Charter Hall (nicknamed Slaughter Hall, Scotland).. Beaufighters? no! Beauforts for a week.

New Years Day and the C.O. took me up and demonstrated the Beaufighter. For this you stood behind him in a well on a trap door and watched over his shoulder, no dual. A further demonstration the next day by another pilot on the single engine approach. Standing there I could see the sweat running down the back of his neck and concluded he was not too happy about a single engined approach. When he closed the one throttle there appeared a plan view of the runway, I got the feeling of being in a runaway lift, this was followed by a hell of a crunch when we hit the runway, what happened next I am not sure, as I was in a heap on the floor, but I must admit he was very considerate, he said "You cannot go solo in this one, it needs an undercarriage check, I will find you another -Good luck".. Full of confidence you take a Beaufighter up for the first time. You then transfer to B Squadron and sort out a radar operator from those swanning around.

January 1945, airborne at last with your own crew, February, Air Firing Course, good, above average, not so good was a complaint from the armourers"- that is the second time you have shot that drogue off, we have to walk miles looking in the fields for it.

At last Mosquito's and a short Intruder course which included some semi operational flying over the North Sea identifying 'bogies', mostly returning Lancs. Good 27th April 45 you are signed off as a fully qualified night fighter pilot. Not so good, a few weeks later Hitler jacks it in (I still think he knew I was coming). Good you are going to 89 Squadron in the Far East. Not so good, you have to do a Jungle Survival course in Bhopal, which includes four of you drawing fifty sterilising water tablets and being put down in the jungle somewhere to find your own food and a way home. You are aware of course that this is the Madhya Pradesh some of the finest tiger hunting country in India, so you are not surprised when you see a large specimen tiger standing on the path you want to use, you just do the normal thing and have an accident with no laundry around. I must admit it was a beautiful animal, especially as it loped away in the other direction. You have been taught the valuable lesson of extracting excrement from the water from semi dried up river beds before you put the sterilising tablets in, when you feel really thirsty, you find it tastes like drinking the local swimming bath water.

So now the Japs have also packed it in. Never mind, leaflets are being dropped over Sumatra saying the Dutch are coming back. Hold on, the wings of one of our Mosquito's has dropped off in mid air, right over the runway. So in February you get the job of testing repaired aircraft from the M.U.. Then in February 46 the squadron is disbanded and becomes 22 Squadron awaiting Brigands. No more retraining for me, I am due for demob, Home Sweet Home.

This turned out to be a 'cruise' in an aircraft carrier. We did have four three day stops for repairs in Columbo, Port Said and Gibraltar, shore leave every time as the Captain was an ex-Fleet Air Arm pilot.

I still think my claim to being one of the highest trained pilots in the RAF, at that time, still stands.

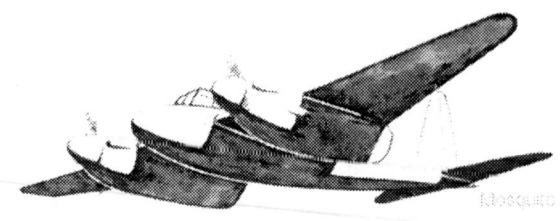

One last duty was to go to the London Zoo and make sure Vicky, an Himalayan Bear, our Squadron mascot, who had been sent to the Zoo in a Sunderland some weeks before, had arrived safely. She had and answered to her name, but gave me the bird when she realised I had not got a bottle of beer for her, her nightly tipple at Seletar.

A CHANCE MEETING.

By F/Lt. E.L. Jones DFC.

Shortly after I left the Royal Air Force in January 1948 I joined the RAFVR club whose headquarters were in South Street, London. .Every year they held an annual dinner which I used to attend with friends. Douglas Bader was always at the top table and always gave his usual rumbustious speech.

Membership diminished and the club left South Street to share headquarters with the Royal Naval club in Hill Street. Then, eventually, the club folded and was disbanded. Looking around for something to replace the VR. Club I heard of the Bomber Command Annual Reunion Dinner at the Grosvenor House Hotel which was always graced by the presence of "Bomber" Harris our well loved wartime chief.

E Jones Second from Left

One year I decided to attend and requested to sit at the 49 Squadron table. This was probably around 1970 .I was hoping to meet at least one squadron contemporary. The fellow sitting opposite me had a white beard and flew

Wapitis in some remote country. No luck there and then another fellow chipped in with his stories about Hampdens - still no luck. However, as luck would have it the fellow sitting next to me was indeed on the squadron at the same time as myself.

We started swapping 49 Squadron flying tales and I eventually got round to telling him of a particular incident in which I was partly involved. It was the night of 10/11 November 1943 when we were briefed to go to the Modane Tunnel located on the frontier between France and Italy. The idea was to break it up to prevent the passage of German troops to and from the Italian front. We were all very excited about this one. All our trips to date were against heavily defended German targets but this was a French target and, by comparison, should be a `doddle` - we hoped.

We were queuing up for take off, I was something like 7th or 8th in the queue when something happened out there on the runway. We couldn't see what the trouble was. Fiskerton's main runway was not level and the final few hundred yards was obscured by the slight rise in the runway. The four Merlin engines, each idling at 1000 revs eliminated any outside noise. We were told the raid was off and the Lancasters still awaiting take off were diverted back to their dispersals.

Myself and my crew along with many others were pretty cheesed off with this turn of events. We were robbed of what turned out to be our only French target. We must have been firm asleep when, some hours later, there was a terrific explosion which apparently distributed parts of a Lancaster over a wide area. We anticipated the worst and assumed some of our aircraft had bought it. Details of this never did filter back to our flight, it was not a crew from our own A Flight and at the time that was all that mattered. And so life on the Squadron carried on, as normal as life on a squadron could be. So I told this story to the pilot sitting next to me and to my utter amazement he said "Guess what - I was piloting that Lanc".

The meal must have been getting cold but the wine was disappearing fast as Ernest Webb unfolded the actual happenings of that night some twenty years previous. It was the night of 10/11 November 1943 and the target was the Modane Tunnel as Ernest lined up his Lancaster P Peter on the main runway. Slowly advancing the four throttles until they were through "the gate" the Lanc gradually gathered speed. Suddenly Ernest became aware of his starboard wing looming large in his cabin window and almost immediately, without warning his port undercarriage collapsed. P Peter slewed off the runway at speed narrowly missing the Watch Tower and finally finished up pointing in the direction from which it had just come. Small fires were already licking around the aircraft as Ernest dived out of his own sliding window. The fuselage had split into two sections and the rear turret had been thrown clear with the rear gunner still trapped inside, his flying boot was caught in the wreckage but with a quick twist and a tug Ernest was able to free him. By now the Blood Waggon had arrived complete with the Station Medical Officer

A head count showed that there were still two members of the crew missing. Ignoring the 303 ammunition exploding all around the aircraft, Ernest and the M.O. dived back into the aircraft only to discover that the two missing men were nowhere to be seen. Eventually they turned up, apparently, as soon as the aircraft came to rest they scrambled out and ran at high speed into the darkness with the live bombs very much in mind.

It was some hours later when there was a violent explosion and pieces of P Peter were deposited over a wide area. All that was left of the aircraft was a single key which is still one of the proudest possessions of the lucky pilot.

The five aircraft which managed to get airborne were, on their return, diverted to Dunholme Lodge. Bomber Command lost no aircraft in the air that night but they did lose one on the ground.

I have since forgiven Ernest for robbing us of that French trip. He survived his tour and we are the best of friends meeting annually at our 49 Squadron reunions in Lincolnshire.

Editors Note

Was this the occasion when, allegedly, Douglas Bader got up to speak at a London function and Eric Morecombe, at a nearby table said, "Good Lord, look who's here, it's Kenneth Moore" The audience erupted and even Douglas Bader had the good grace to laugh

Mascot

"WE FLEW IN FORTS"

By Alan Mercer

It was in November 1944 that another bomber crew was starting to be formed as we came together at No.11 Operational Training Unit, at Westcott & Oakley, Bucks.

We were F/O. Ken Kemmett Pilot, Sgt. Alan Mercer Navigator, F/O. "Lofty" Baumfield (NZ) B/A, F/Sgt. Steve Spregg W/OP, Sgt. "Duke" Maddox (NZ) R/AG, and Sgt. "Curly" Herlihy (NZ) MU/AG; Ken was about 23 years old, Steve starting his second tour of ops. was about 30, the rest of us were around 20 years old.

Some fourteen weeks later and some 87 hours flying in Wellingtons found ourselves a "qualified" bomber crew, with the experience of being diverted to other airfields, landing at Newmarket racecourse (gate crashing an Army dance dressed in our flying clothing) Calling for assistance from Darky (night time emergency radio network) because our navigation aids had packed up, and we were close to Rugby radio masts about 1200 ft high, with a cloud base lower than that. We were guided into Polebrook, a USAAF airbase, given supper in a "film set" dining hall, sleeping in hospital beds as there were no other empty beds. Memories of walking miles in snow to go to local pubs, coming back to a Nissen hut with a white hot stove in the middle, ideal for toast after an evening at a pub or trying to open a soldered tin containing cake sent for the Kiwis in our crew.

A satisfying period of training (and other life) marred only by the news that my friend Eric Thurston had been killed in a mid air collision at another OTU in Scotland. However at course end, our Pilot told us that we had been posted to a special duties squadron in Norfolk. We arrived there, RAF Oulton nr Aylsham, I think we were picked up from Norwich railway station and driven to Oulton. Just outside the airfield was the scattered remains of a crashed B-17 Flying Fortress, shot down by a German intruder a night or two previously, not the best of welcomes! (I learned some years later that 8 of the crew were killed in that crash and met one of the survivors, an AG at a reunion in 1994).

Before joining the Squadron, we had to spend four weeks at No.1699 Heavy Conversion Unit, also at RAF Oulton, gaining two more AGs, Freddie Langhorn and "Chalky" White, 18 year old Sgts, plus Sgt"Smithy"Smith, Flight Engineer and P/O "Olly"Green, Special Radar Operator in our crew. One of the staff pilots at the Con unit was Murrey Peden who checked our crew, he wrote a very good book called "A Thousand Must Fall".

Alan Mercer. Front row, third from left.

It was the beginning of April 1945 before we joined 214 Squadron. A week was spent pottering about, then our first operation to Schleswig Holstein on a spoof raid, dropping window, and jamming German RDF etc. We learned a few days later, in an intelligence report, that a squadron of German night fighters had taken off to come after our few Fortresses (looking like a large number of bombers on the German Radar) that was one lot of night fighters less going after the main force which was our raison d'être.

What an experience that first op was! The B/A and myself attended a separate navigation briefing almost like a classroom exercise or exam. with our routes mapped out etc. Then we dined on the traditional aircrew supper, fried egg, bacon and chips, not the best pre flight meal but eggs were a luxury in wartime. Afterwards we went to the Sgts Mess where I brought out two half pints of beer as a mock bravado gesture of insurance against us not coming back. An hour later, drawing our parachutes, Mae West's etc a ride in a truck to dispersal, pee on the back wheel, finally getting airborne around sunset. Another hour, we were over Germany (not much left of opposition as the invasion was going well but still plenty of night-fighters left). My navigation equipment was working perfectly, a bit of jamming on the Gee set but still clear pulses to give me position fixes. The gunners reported vapour trails, we were flying at 22,000ft, puzzling because our squadron aircraft were flying at staggered intervals about 20 miles behind each other. Obvious conclusion? Then some searchlights came near to us, so our skipper started to weave, well I reckon that we actually corkscrewed for half an hour. I was airsick for the first (and only) time in my life, fried egg and chips etc beer, and butterflies transferred rapidly from my stomach to one of the spare charts rather neatly and with my oxygen mask back on, I was then able to carry on. Six of the other crew were also sick, but at least we were still alive.

On one op, cruising fairly calmly at 22,000ft there was a burst of gunfire from the Mid Upper, the Pilots reaction was to stand the plane on its nose and lose a few thousand feet straight away. The M/U then apologised! claiming to have caught his parachute harness in the triggers, which did not have trigger guards. We all reckoned that he had fallen asleep, waking up with a jerk, thus catching his harness that way.

The Flying Fortress was chosen for Radar Counter Measures for a number of reasons; it could fly high, (Stirling's previously used had a difficult job to get much above 15,000ft). It had a spacious compartment for the W/Op and Special Operator together with their radar receivers and transmitters, also the internal bomb bays were an ideal shape and size for the pillar-box sized transmitters we carried for jamming purposes. The Rear Gunner had a very tight squeeze towards the rear with only a saddle type seat to sit on for the total time airborne. Further forward, the Mid Upper Gunner had a reasonable position and of course the Pilot and Engineer enjoyed armchair comfort (?) The B/A and myself had our little office in the nose, a chart table 3ft by 2ft, with the Gee set to the left, Air Position Indicator (Heath Robinson box of gears and cogs, but it worked), and H2S (radar picture of the ground, fine but Germans could home onto it) on the right hand side of the table. The B/A worked on some Radar gear when we reached the target area so we had no need to look out, our windows were curtained, and we declined the Pilots' suggestion to look out, as we were too cosy to bother about the war outside. The B/A and I had to stand behind the Pilot and Engineer for takeoffs and landings and one night returning from an op, I saw the red exhaust flames of a plane crossing in front of us from left to right, slightly above us about twenty feet away. "Not one of ours" said the skipper sticking the nose down to touch the runway quicker. The only time I had seen the enemy and only 2 seconds separated us from being in his gun sight.

On one of our air tests, I had a look back from the astro-dome at the Pilot, Engineer, and behind them, the Mid Upper Gunner who, naturally had a very good view all around, Curly depressed his guns and fired at me, well perhaps 12 inches above the astral-dome, I couldn't help ducking! Another time on an air test, he test fired his guns, then against the rules, he centralised his guns rearward before clearing a live round from the breech block, the live round cooking in the hot gun went off hitting our own tail about 12 inches above the Rear A/G's head. The Pilot wasn't told until after landing and wasn't amused at the news; he had felt that the controls had become stiff during landing. Sometimes I would join the two waist gunners for take off and try to keep my head out of their side window but as speed increased I had to give way, and get my head back in.

On another occasion, whilst sitting around on the grass at the dispersal point, dressed in our flying clothing, waiting for take off time, another Fortress's waist gun started firing, it appeared that their Waist Gunner had left his gun strap on the gun trigger so that the vibration of the engines starting up swung

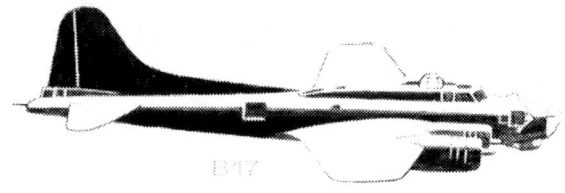

the gun around and pulled the strap tight on the trigger. That episode was good for a laugh just before take off.

Some of the lighter parts of living on the airfield were very good, there was a large lake in the grounds of nearby Blickling Hall, ideal for dinghy drill practice, especially as the Spring weather was getting better. We found that swimming around the lake towing the dinghy made better speed than paddling the dinghy in the approved manner. Afterwards, we used the showers in the officer's quarters, which were in the grounds, to wash the pond weed off ourselves. Our NZ B/A had a visit from his brother Ben in the NZ navy; we found Sgts uniform for Lofty and his brother so that we could all eat together in the Sgts Mess.

I had a go at flying the Fort. (I'd had the controls of a Tiger Moth Anson, and Wimpey before) doing reasonably well despite wisecracks from the Rear A/G, but losing patience with him, I started kicking the rudder bar to and fro which must have knocked his head in a similar manner to and fro inside his small headroom. I wasn't allowed to continue the treatment for long, as the Skipper took control back again.

We had a fire during an air test once, well a lot of smoke anyway, one of the electric motors in the bomb bay started giving off a lot of smoke, so a couple of us went to town with the fire extinguishers and put out the smoke by the time we landed. On these air tests, we were supposed to take our parachutes with us and usually we did so as a matter of course. It was amusing to see that the two crew members who did not bother to take their 'chutes had the whitest of faces while the rest of us could see the joke.

At our working altitude of 20,000ft we obviously were on oxygen, the oxygen mask after a couple of hours began to chafe our faces and it was quite a relief to take it off for a few seconds in order to have a quick swig of coffee from the Thermos or a bite of a sandwich neatly wrapped in newspaper. There was always a drop of condensation falling from the mask and this dropped to form a blob of ice on the chart until we returned to a lower altitude and thawed out, then the chart became rather soggy in places. We had electrically heated flying suits and what with plugging that in, plus the oxygen, plus the intercom, and our seat belts, I was well trained for the car seat belt laws of later years.

Life on the Squadron was easy, if we had been flying the night before, then we didn't book in until about mid-day at our sections, otherwise we signed in normally, around 9am had a chat, looked at notices, maybe an odd lecture. A few minutes away from the Nav section were the camp gates, always open and a village PO/General shop/tea room providing a meeting place as an alternative to the NAAFI wagon. If a few days had elapsed since an op or exercise, then the Navs had to see the Nav Leader who had marked our charts and duly praised or criticised our performance.

We, the NCOs shared a Nissen hut with the NCOs of two other crews; one crew had come with us from O.T.U., the other crew failed to return one night. When we woke up in the morning, there were five or six empty beds, later in the day their belongings had been cleared out.

My late arrival on an operational Squadron, flying only 3 operations was a very good reason for surviving the war, some 8 Fortresses were lost from 214 Squadron in the last three months of the war (some 60 lives lost). Let us not forget that some 55,000 other lads in Bomber Command also failed to make it, whilst some 70,000 came through more or less OK.

On the 22nd April 1945, our crew was scheduled as standby, this meant extra work for me as Navigator, and I had to prepare three flight plans in case we had to take the place of any of the other crews. Supper, the flying gear, etc. and out to dispersal to wait and see if we were required or not. All the aircraft took off all right so we were able to go back to whatever we wanted to do! I had three useless flight plans, left to tear up!!!

By this time our Pilot had got his second ring (F/Lt), Steve got his commission after W/O, and we senior Sgts became F/Sgts, the Skipper did nag me to apply for a commission the same as Steve, but I felt that my W/O would be due soon and it wasn't worth while becoming an officer for the "short time" before I was demobbed. A W/O Navigator was paid more than a P/O and about the same as a F/O.

V.E. Day came. We celebrated on the airfield. An ox or sheep was roasted on a spit. We had some beer, I think! I don't remember much of that evening. The next day, we elected for a quiet evening at the pictures, our usual mode of transport was by bike, and if our issued bike had been taken we took the nearest one or doubled up on one bike. Returning to camp, sitting on the handlebars of Chalky's bike, we met 2 WAAFs riding bikes, and we became "tangled". I ended up in hospital with concussion! Nevertheless, I returned to flying in 4 weeks.

After the war ended we had a lot of surplus ammunition to dispose of, a flight over the North Sea, open bomb doors and so we dropped it, there was a catwalk through the bomb bay for us to walk from front to rear etc and it felt strange to stand on an 18"gangway a few hundred feet above the sea below our feet. Coming back from this little task we found a Lancaster had formated beside us, after exchanging the usual victory signals, the Lanc shut off one engine and then started pulling away from us despite our Pilot trying to push our throttles as hard as he could, the Lanc continued on three engines to leave us well behind.

We took part in a couple of exercises in July called Post Mortem, to test the effectiveness of the German Radar, flying up and down the North Sea and in and out of Denmark. One of those flights was 7 1/2 hours, the longest time I had been airborne in the RAF (but nothing to compare with the Catalina).
The Squadron split up, I went to a Transport Squadron on Stirling's for a while, taking mail and newspapers across to the troops in Germany. Then 1946, a wasted year, marking time, waiting for demob.

Our crew kept in touch on and off over the years except poor Olly, he was posted to India, had a joyride in a Beaufighter which stalled on takeoff in January 1947.

Around 1979 Lofty came here from New Zealand, and we had a very good get-together in a restaurant just outside Gloucester. In 1985, I went to NZ, met up with Lofty, Duke and Curly, then a few years later went down to Plymouth and saw Kemmett, so I can say that in that period of time I had seen every crew member either in mini reunions here or in NZ. Photographs from those occasions were put together to make up a composite picture of the crew as we were in 1945.

Freddie died in August 1981; Steve about a year later, then the news came from New Zealand that curly died in Nov 1992, shortly followed by Duke in April 1993. I visited Kemmett in May 1993 when he joked about his replacement heart valve being time expired, he died a month later.

In 1994, three of us went back to Oulton for a Reunion evening in Aylsham Town Hall (one ex WAAF M/T driver claimed to remember us all). Next day, a service at the church beside Blicking Hall, lunch at the Buckinghamshire Arms, and then the dedication of the Memorial Plaque at the airfield. Afterwards a walk around some of the remaining old buildings, with a photograph of nearly thirty ex 214 aircrew. At the end of the day, we went to Oulton Hall for refreshments in a marquee in the grounds, there I met up with my Flight Commander, Sqn/ Ldr. Bob Davies and asked him to sign my log-book (again after 49 years). Smithy died in March 1995, Lofty died in August 2000, leaving Chalky and myself in England out of our crew of 10 in 1945.

Memories of firm friendships remain.

31 SQUADRON, 205 GROUP
SOUTH AFRICAN AIR FORCE

Wartime experiences
From 13th July to 13th November 1944

By K C Jones

We, the Franklin crew, consisting of Captain Reg Franklin, Pilot; Lt. Lou Moller, Navigator; 2nd Lt. "Shortie" Rudham, Wireless Op. Sgt. Chris Botha, Engineer all S.A.A.F. Sgt. Ken Jones, Bomb Aimer; Sgt. Bill Williams, Air Gunner and Sgt. "Nick" Nickerson, all R.A.F., arrived at Celone, Foggia, Italy, at approximately 6pm on 13th July 1944.

We were directed to the barrack store, where we received two blankets each. Then we, the four Sergeants, were allocated a tent that had not been erected. The first thing we did, was to set about erecting it, but daylight intervened and we did not finally complete it but it was habitable. Proceeding then to the mess, we had a meal of tinned meat and vegetable (M&V), dehydrated potatoes and a mug of tea. This was to be our staple diet for the next three months.

After a tiring day it was time to "turn in". The question now was how we were going to sleep, as no beds were issued, so we finally agreed, that each of us should "chip in" one of our two blankets to lay on the ground and using our kit bags as pillows, cover up with the remaining blanket. Thus we turned in.

During the night it deluged rain with inevitable consequences as the tent was pitched on a slope and water leaked through soaking the blanket on the floor.

I happened to be nearest to the leak and immediately roused the other three. We all got up, dressed and stood up for the rest of the night from 3am till daybreak. Welcome to Celone!

The following day, Chris organised a 3 ton truck to visit the American Lightning fighter squadron, based further along the road from Celone, where there were some wooden long range fuel tank boxes available. From these we reconstructed a "Five star" tent, complete with wooden floor, kitchen and ablution facilities. This proved to be the envy of the Squadron and most couldn't wait for us to go so they could move in.

Our operational duties, flying Liberators, got off to a bad start because we had to return to base due to bad weather on 21st and 23rd July. The third trip, however, on 26th July, was to be over that heavily defended target, the dreaded Ploesti Oil Refinery in Rumania, where the Americans had a hard time during their daylight sorties. We, of course, raided it at night but it was equally well defended with plenty of flack around. I am not sure how many aircraft we lost that night, I think the Squadron got away reasonably intact. The following night we raided the Oil Refinery at Prahova and again the losses were light, as far as I can remember.

Following a couple of raids on a Marshalling Yard at Valence, France and Szombatheley Landing Ground in Greece, we were despatched to lay mines along the Danube. This entailed low level flying, so low in fact, that as we flew along the valley, the most significant fact I remember was the ack-ack being directed downwards upon us. Fortunately no one got hit that night, so I can only assume that the maximum angle of depression of the guns was higher than that required to obtain the right trajectory to hit us.

The fourth mission, on the night of 13th /14th August was shrouded in mystery, we could not find out where it was to be. All we were told at the briefing was that we were to fly with full tanks of fuel and empty bomb bays to Brindisi, to receive our full briefing and to pick up our load from there. The only thing we did know at that point was that it was to he a long run, because our fuel load was at maximum capacity. We soon found out that it was to be supply dropping over Warsaw, Poland, to the Peoples Army, of General Bor Komerowski`s uprising in that city. Without exception, everyone was surprised at such an operation, as it entailed 10 to 11 hours flying over enemy territory, without escort or Pathfinders. To add to the danger, we were briefed to go in over the target at 400 feet, with flaps down to reduce the speed to 120 m.p.h; to pin point the specific dropping area and deliver the containers with accuracy, so that the enemy could not take advantage of them. Imagine then, what sitting targets we were for the ack-ack gunners. We were one of the lucky ones, because of the eleven aircraft the Squadron put up that night, only four returned.

Later it was officially stated that the operation was in the same category as the Dam Busters. What the skipper and I had agreed before our run-in was, after release of the containers, we should climb up to 12,000 feet and race for home. Unfortunately, after about 10 minutes of flight, the rear gunner piped up " Cats Eyes", this meant that German night fighters were after us. This was a system whereby, a tracking station on the ground picked up our track and had marked it with a flare. They would continue tracking us and after about 30 seconds, they would put up another flare immediately behind our aircraft. Meanwhile, a J.U. 88 night fighter would home in on this for the kill, with the inevitable result. We had cause to be grateful to that gunner because, due to his alertness, we started to weave the aircraft, to break up the track. We had this situation for about an hour, playing cat and mouse, because each time we returned to our intended track, the same performance ensued.

Altogether the round trip took us 10hrs. 55mins; we had taken off at sunset and landed at base at sunrise. The whole affair had been a nightmare.

It is significant to note here, that two things happened as a result of this operation, we had to virtually rebuild the Squadron with aircraft, and sadly with men. The Polish Government in Exile awarded those who took part with the Polish Cross of Valour. Additionally, the Peoples Army Cross, [A.KA] and the Cross of Warsaw [KW], were also awarded for this dangerous exploit.

After raids carried out on marshalling yards, which seemed to be a speciality, oil refineries, road/railway bridges and troop concentrations, another hard target stands out in my memory, the ball bearing factory at Niblunger Werke in Austria. It was heavily defended and we were glad to get out of there with no mishaps to us, but several got hit that night with one or two losses.

Another incident I can remember was the weather deteriorating whilst on the way to a target whilst flying over Yugoslavia. When we left base at Celone, the weather was fairly good, so I thought I would get into the front gun turret to do some map reading. I was locked in by the navigator so that I could rotate the turret for good observation. All went well until we entered the Yugoslave territory, when the weather began to deteriorate. After about 15 minutes of flying, the cloud was so thick I could not see to map read. I sat there waiting for us to fly out of the clouds. Suddenly the aircraft dropped the port wing, followed by the nose and we literally fell out of the sky in a banked dive. The pilot and engineer were struggling with the controls to right the plane but to no avail, it would not respond to corrective action. Down we came, in this uncomfortable attitude, engines screaming and with 10.000lbs of bombs on board. Needless to say we were all frightened to death, I know I was. The stupid things you think when facing certain death, in my mind I thought being locked in the front turret I would hit the ground first, I would he killed first and then blown up with the bombs. However, it was not to be because, having fallen out of control from 11,000ft, to just under 2,000ft, the aircraft began to judder gently at first, then increasing in intensity until I thought it was going to be shaken to pieces. At this point, the port wing picked up and shot over to starboard but was brought level by the pilot. The cause of this phenomenon was that we had flown into a vacuum, made by two fronts causing a down-draught between them. It is an experience I do not recommend.

Our next target that I can recollect was on 10th September 1944 where we were directed to bomb the marshalling yard at Milan, Northern Italy, with 12, 500lb incendiary cluster bombs. This was the main German assembly point for supplies en-route to the Kesselring army holding up the Allied advance in central Italy. As we arrived in the target area. it was covered by cloud. I could see target marker flares dropped by the Pathfinders that were all over the place, giving no clear definition as to where the target actually was. I must point out here, that when a target was covered with cloud, it was customary to drop bombs by lining up on these target markers as they were usually fairly accurately placed. As I was in doubt and in charge of the aircraft at this point, I cleared with the navigator that there was no high ground and then asked the pilot to descend 1,000 ft to see if we could break cloud. This we did five times until at about 7,000 ft we finally broke cloud and I had a wonderful sight of the target. I turned, and there laid out in front of me was the huge marshalling yard with fires burning around the periphery. I could see trains pulling trucks and lots of trucks parked in sidings. I turned the aircraft onto the target to drop my 12-500 Ibs incendiary bombs, but just as I was running up for release, someone just ahead of me put a stick diagonally across the target, straddling the railway lines and causing trucks to burst into flames, a wonderful sight and a real picture book perfect bombing run. I thought to myself, hold on mate, there is another load on its way to you, and as I looked back my bombs landed with the same effect. I have often wondered who that other bomb-aimer was, and whether Kesselring wondered where some of his supplies of ammunition went

It was on the marshalling yard raid on Trieste that we received our only damage through enemy action. At the briefing, we were told what the air defences were like and that we would encounter very light opposition, mostly light ack-ack from mobile guns. When we arrived the barrage was the worst we had experienced anywhere and we got hit in the port outer engine. With oil spewing everywhere it suddenly died, so we feathered the propeller [turning the pitch of the blade edge on to the air flow to reduce drag] and flew to base on the remaining three engines, quite easily really with an empty aircraft.

Our last operation was a rare daylight sortie. The Germans were retreating from Greece and were reforming defences at a place called Podgorica in Southern Yugoslavia. Intelligence required us to bomb it as Tito had evacuated the local population so it was all clear to saturate the whole town. We arrived over target with a bombing time of five minutes and then to get out fast, in case of fighter attack in that area so close to Greece. For us it was a bit of a disaster because when I opened the bomb bay doors, ran up on target and pressed the bomb release button, only four of the twelve bombs left the racks. The usual drill was, to make a quarter turn and fly over the target again and try to drop the rest. I advised the pilot to do this, but on pressing the release button, only three more left the racks. Bombing time had now expired but I advised the pilot to turn for a last attempt, this he did reluctantly. On this attempt I decided to press the jettison release lever but only another two went. By this time, the ack-ack opened up at our solitary aircraft still flying around, so I decided that enough was enough and I told the skipper to head on out for home amongst cheers and such comments as "about …..time too".

We now had three bombs hung up on the racks, so I decided I would drop them safe over the Adriatic Sea on the way back and advised the pilot accordingly. To get these bombs off their hooks meant going into the bomb bay and releasing them by hand. The bombs were dispersed two in the forward bay and one in the rear bay of the starboard side. To release them manually I had to walk along a catwalk only 9ins. wide, reach up to the units, disengage the arming wires and prise open the release levers for each bomb. This was done without a parachute and standing on a narrow catwalk with bomb bay doors wide open and nothing between me and fresh air. To be honest I found it quite disturbing. However, this had to be done for the safety of the aircraft and the crew, because to land with bombs still on board and no idea why they hung up, may have caused them to release as we landed and blown us all up and damage the runway into the bargain.

Another little tale of the organisation is that it was customary for what we called the "Booze Wagon" to visit us every Wednesday. This was arranged by Mrs Jan Smuts, wife of the then President of South Africa. When it arrived they handed out, amongst other things, liqueurs and spirits for re-stocking the Officers', Sergeants' and O.Rs' messes. There was never any beer. One day our rear gunner came in and announced that he had been over to the American camp and he had struck a deal with them, if we could let them have a couple of bottles of whisky, then they would give us a crate of bottled beer in exchange. The deal was on, so over to the mess we went and sent him over with them. I must say that I have never enjoyed a beer so much.

The story related in Neil Orpen's book "Betrayed" is a true record, it was the Franklin crew who did it. We went to the aircraft servicing section and acquired the old inner tubes to make into catapults. We sat there for about a couple of hours shooting stones at pigeons, they were so profuse that even the poorest shot could hardly miss them. Incidentally, the pigeon pie we managed to get the cook to make was delicious after the tinned meat and vegetable and de-hydrated potatoes we had eaten in abundance.

Regarding personalities, crews generally stuck together and somehow we tended not to mix too much. Having said that, there were a few with whom we had trained earlier and we would visit one another tents, or see in the mess for a chat etc. There was one named Rogers, [known to me as Rog, for short], we had trained together at No. 43 Air School, Port Alfred, South Africa, unfortunately he met his fate whilst standing in for me. When we were rebuilding the Squadron after the Warsaw episode there was an influx of new crews, and It was the practice to screen the pilots and bomb-aimers when performing their first operation.

On this occasion, the Franklin crew were on stand down, so I was detailed to screen one of the new bomb- aimers. When I reported to the ops. room I was detailed to round up the Franklin crew to report in as we were to carry out this operation, therefore, I went back into my own crew. At the same time, I also brought Rog with me as requested by the briefing officer to take my place with the new bomb aimer. There were gathering thunder clouds during take off, and by the time the end of the queue came to get air borne it was virtually overhead. Rog was one of the last to take off and flew into one of these clouds and was struck by lightning. The plane just blew up. Sadly, a new crew on their first op, and Rog, a dear friend, were lost. To this day I still feel guilty as it could so easily have been me.

Reg Franklin, the skipper, was a good pilot, in that he was very careful and had done one tour of ops, in the desert of North Africa. A tribute is fitting to him for bringing us through. It is significant to note that we, the Franklin

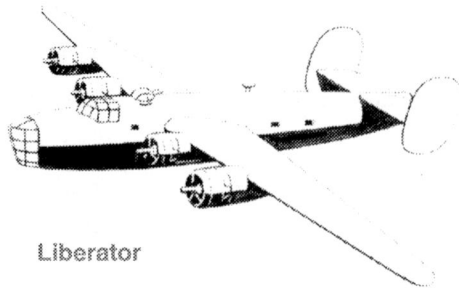
Liberator

crew of "V" victor aircraft, were the first and only crew of 31 Squadron S.A.A F, to completely finish a full tour of operations, such were the losses. The Commanding Officer, Lt, COL Nel. was an amiable man, each evening whilst marshalling for take off, he would come to each aircraft and wish us good luck, an act which endeared him to us. In 1991, I had the good fortune to meet up with my tail gunner again, after a period of 47 years. Since then I have visited him several times each year and of course we talk about those times and wonder how we managed to come through it all.

These then are just some of my experiences, whilst serving on 31 South African Air Force Squadron, at Celone, Italy in 1944.

A FLIGHT TO REMEMBER.

By Flt/Sgt D J Venning 620 Sqdn 38 Group

It was some time in January 1945 and we were stationed at Great Dunmow, Essex flying Stirlings. Our crew was, J. (Buggy) Harrison, Pilot, Freddie Jutsum, Nav, Jim Viney BJA, Henry Rowland, W/op/Ag, Fred Dunne, R/Gnr, Doug Venning, F/Engr. It was a period of poor weather and we had flown on some exercise having taken off after lunch but on this occasion had a passenger, an Aussie W/0p. who wanted to add some hours to his Log.

We had completed our job and were approaching base at circuit height when the weather clamped rapidly and we were in snow. We called the tower who advised us "not to land but stay on circuit and we will get you down". Fine and almost immediately we hit violent slipstream twice so Buggy said "We are not staying here it`s too b--- dicey". So, he turned on a reciprocal, standard procedure, and we climbed a little for safety but could not clear the snowstorm. We flew on and turned 90 and then 180 degrees but to no avail, what next? We`ll have to climb above it and see where we are, since at this stage we weren't exactly sure of our location due to the very strong winds. We called base for a report on the conditions, no answer. R.T was out, so we climbed.

At 9,000 feet, still in cloud and snow our instruments disappeared and no vacuum to drive the B.F.Panel. We were picking up ice rapidly and our cabin heating shut off, which was found due to large pinnacles of ice covering the air intakes that passed through the exhaust stubs for heating. Almost immediately our A.S.I. packed up despite the heater being on. Now we were really flying by the seat of our skipper's pants. (I was reminded recently at a crew luncheon that I apparently rigged up a plumb line by tying a spanner to a piece of string and hanging this assembly from the cockpit roof to help the skipper remain at a safe angle and attitude). We reached 13,000 feet and things were really desperate so we offered our passenger the opportunity to bale out. He thought seriously and said "OK." and I started to open the hatch when Jim, up front yelled, "We are breaking cloud" Our passenger held fast. Within a few minutes Jim again yelled "There`s a hole in the clouds going all the way down".

Hope at last. We had probably reached our ceiling with the amount of ice we had picked up, we were frozen and had no oxygen, this was the highest we had ever flown. We had to use the opportunity to get down and fortunately the "hole" was large enough for us to maintain a tight turn whilst rapidly descending. Some way down Jim again yelled " There`s an airfield below us, keep going down as we are" which we did. The escape hatch was now in place again and our Aussie friend smiled a little. We tried but still no R/T despite the better air in the hole. Now we could see the airfield but we knew not where, but who cared, an airfield is an airfield when in trouble.

We continued virtually down to circuit height and could identify P51 Mustangs and felt a little happier, still no response to R/T so we came in to land, fast because we had no A.S.I. As we approached on our final, tower broke through with "Lancaster, you are free to land" All eyes available looked for the Lanc - to no avail. We touched down feeling very relieved and as we reached the end of the runway our Gunner said "There`s a Fortress just touching down, turn off as soon as we can" We parked. The Fortress parked just behind us in the same pan and looked very small both to us and it's crew who also insisted on calling us a Lanc, we, The Queen of the Skies, such ignorance. The Fort had made a forced landing.

We learned on "reporting in" that we had landed at a USAAC base of escort Mustangs whose days work had finished but we were just in time to enjoy a good meal of pork chops etc, despite the molasses poured on top. The base was Wormingsford, also in Essex and only about 22 miles from our own base. We reported in by telephone and requested some ground staff to help sort out our problems. They arrived next morning by truck and we found more trouble than we had anticipated, particularly, the Magnetos had iced up. Our Aussie friend departed on the next truck back to base but our ground crew returned two days later to finish the job. In all we stayed on base at Wormingsford for 8 days when we flew our kite back to base and with no recriminations on our safe return. It had been a cold 8 days since we only had battle-dress to wear but the food was excellent.

A flight to remember? Certainly, but we also remembered the cuisine.

CAN WE HAVE OUR MONEY BACK

Doug Venning.

It wasn't quite as the title suggests but the war in Europe was over and the Bank of England was holding large sums of frozen assets belonging to most European countries who clearly needed their assets to commence a rebuilding programme. From memory it was only a couple of weeks after VE Day when our crew were detailed to fly to Colerne, near Bath, to stay overnight. We would be briefed for our mission on arrival at Colerne.

Doug Venning. Third from left back row

We duly landed and found the station accupied by a Czech Meteor Squadron and a host of British troops. "What gives?" we asked. A couple of other Stirlings arrived from our Squadron and we were duly marshalled in to a briefing room. We were to fly to Prague next morning and return to our station on completion of our job.

Gardamoen Airfield Norway. JU88 `s behind Stirling

The following morning we were met at our aircraft by an escort of the Czech Army, one captain, one Lieutenant and one Sergeant, all armed These were to travel with us and our freight and to stay with it on arrival. Next a large black van from the Bank of England arrived and loaded some large coffin like crates on board our 'plane, closely watched by our escort. Inside the crates? about £5,000,000 of gold bullion, part of the frozen assets of Czechoslovakia now being returned despite being occupied by Russia.

The flight went well and where possible we followed the East/West Autobahns some of the way but we had very few detailed maps of Prague to lead us to the airfield. However, our escorts were in the cockpit searching for the first sight of their beloved Prague which they sighted from afar, pointing and saying "See the spires, the airfield is over there". So we landed. The airfield looking rather beaten up and with various German and Russian aircraft around. Hangars were badly damaged and we noted prisoners emptying Gerry cans of fuel into the underground storage tanks under armed guard. We proceeded to the parking area being very careful to obey the directions given to us from the ground by means of a Kalashnikov or similar pointing the way. A large lorry arrived and our escort tried to organise with the Russians the unloading of the freight. We were impressed by the way in which all directions were given by the Russians by the use of the gun, often pointing at one's midrift. All were very scruffy and dirty, and, if these were the women what ever were the men like? On completion we were offered a beer and some black bread which we had been instructed to refuse, we had our own rations and so after a quick snack we restarted the engines and proceeded to the take-off point and left Prague.

On the way back we reflected about what happened to our escort? I imagine they were taken out of circulation in the usual Russian manner. The fewer who knew of this operation the better. The gold no doubt went to Moscow for their benefit, it certainly would not have stayed in Prague since the Russians already had a firm grip on Czechoslavakia. One recalls the fate of the Spanish gold sent to Russia for safe keeping in 1937 and never seen again. We had done our job and on reflection, a sad job into which the politicians of the world had dumped our escort friends of only a few hours. We all know how that gold may have been used over the years and the value of the gold quoted earlier was at 1945 prices.

THE LOSS OF STIRLING LK116

Doug Venning

It occurred on the night of 20th March 1945 on the circuit of RAF Great Dunmow. LK116 was being flown by Sqn. Ldr Whitty, 'B' Flight Commander, No.620 Squadron and crew. He and his crew had arrived only a few days earlier as a replacement for Sqn Ldr B Burridge DFC DFM and had done only limited flying of the type required within 38th Group being specialists in troop support operations.

On this night the crew were to practice a night drop of containers at Gt. Sampford, an airfield only a few miles north of Great Dunmow and then return to base, a one hour flight at the most. On return to the circuit at about 1200 feet altitude, the control tower announced 'Bandits in the area' i.e. intruders, and all station lights were extinguished including the circuit and runway lights. The message was relayed to all aircraft in the area also.

Our Bomb Aimer, Jim Viney and I were just leaving our billet on the North side of the airfield to go to the Mess when this occurred and we immediately heard, and saw an aircraft overhead and heading east, the wrong way round the circuit, and he also had his navigation lights on. Jim asked "Is he towing a glider?" We both looked hard because night glider towing was most unusual and realised that there was a plane following the Stirling. Our minds immediately clicked on and we said "Get your lights off, that's a JU88". Almost immediately the JU88 opened fire with cannon and we saw it rake all the way through the plane to the nose causing fires to start in the port wing. It was reported by Control Tower personnel that about this time a crew member said "There is a plane behind us" since the intercom and R/T was switched on. Could it have been the tail gunner? Instructions had recently been issued from Air Ministry that tail gunners should not stay in their turrets for landing due to the risk of injury in the event of a crash. Good advice in view of this event.

The plane, now ablaze, continued straight and level for a while then gradually heeled over to port and dived into the ground, crashing on the east side of the town near the bridge on the Braintree Road, since named 'Stirling Bridge'. Somehow the Flight Engineer got out of the plane, used his parachute and landed in the town where he was found on the steps of The Saracens Head where he was given some much needed tonic and taken back to camp by an RAF vehicle. Two days later for some reason unknown to any of us in our Section, the F/Eng. was posted to Eastchurch, the infamous station where one was posted if designated 'LMF', most peculiar. As the only survivor what had he done wrong?

What was the cause? Was it due to the Air Ministry ruling that the plane was void of any rearward vision since in 38 Group we had no top turrets and without the rear gunner they were blind, and in this case no awareness of the JU88 behind and closing in for the kill? Why was the plane travelling in a reverse circuit direction? The F/Eng. would normally look out of the Astro Dome occasionally during a flight but prior to landing he would be busy on routine and pre landing checks with the pilot, but whose voice did the Control Tower personnel hear?

We never heard much after that night and we will never know the cause officially, perhaps just another 'pilot error' but Jim and I saw it all played out in detail. A sad end to a crew few of us had a chance to meet and get to know.

F/LT. FREDDIE FOX, D.F.M.
FLIGHT ENGINEER. R.A.F.

A comment on his service history from a colleague

Freddie Fox joined the R.A.F. as a boy Apprentice at Halton in 1933, and passed out as a Fitter 2E, entering man's service early in 1941. at a time when the Short Stirling Bomber, the first "Heavy" was introduced into 3 Group, Bomber Command at Oakington as operational but with many teething problems still to be resolved. He was until then a Corporal Fitter 2E working on Spitfires, but was transferred to Oakington and told "Learn all you can about the Stirling so that you can fly them". A programme was established for this training and he and two other "ex Brats", colleagues from Freddie`s own course of 33 were again brought together. The trio then flew as Mechanics in the early days of the Stirling`s development, and on daylight operations also served as a Waist Gunner along side the W/Op.

Freddie`s first Op. was to Brest, probably on the 28th April or the first week of May 1941. Subsequently, when checking the Ops.list one day he discovered a Sgt. Fox listed to fly, and on checking, his Skipper apologised for omitting to advise him of his promotion, also of being awarded his F/Eng. brevet, a completely new aircrew role a replacement for the 2nd.Pilot. Hence was born the F/Engineer, and Freddie was a proud founder member of the clan.

The Halton trio continued on 7 Sqdn. and each completed a tour by the end of which 7 Sqdn. had become the first Pathfinder force under W/Cmdr. Hamish McHaddie. The Halton trio went on rest to 1651 H.C.U. at Waterbeach as Screen Engineers. After a period of rest Freddie and his colleagues were posted back to 3 Group, Freddie to 15 Sqdn which had by then converted to Lancasters, but now in the expanded Pathfinder Force. In this role the trio each completed a 2nd.tour of operations.

Freddie was awarded the D.F.M. and the Polish D.F.C. for special service to Poland and at some time was commissioned as an Officer. Subsequently Freddie transferred to 242 Sqdn Transport Command, flying Stirling Vs and Yorks in the Far East. He also served in H.M. Kings Flight and after all airborne flying was done flew "a desk" as an Engineering Officer, at one time at High Wycombe, living only two doors away from his former boss, Hamish McHaddie.

It was about this time the role of F/Eng. ceased to exist being replaced by the Air Eng. A/C category but keeping alive the E. brevet. Interestingly, after retirement from the R.A.F. the 'trio' met each year for a birthday and I know that they met in Majorca (where one lives) on his 80th birthday in 1997.
Freddie was a proud member of the R.A.F. and a man of whom his colleagues were equally proud.

MEMORIES

By Rex Hurley

In 1945 I was doing my primary flying on P.T 17 A's (Boeing Stearman) biplanes at No.1. BFTS. Terrel, Texas. Many of the instructors were ex-crop dusters and very "seat of the pants" fliers. My own from Louisiana, had that soft Southern drawl and laid- back approach to life, was very good looking with lots of girl friends. He was the acknowledged master of low flying and admitted he was not as good as some of his fellow instructors at aerobatics but if we ever got into a dogfight with any of them he'd head straight for the ground, they rarely followed us and if they did he would lose them. Not surprisingly of the four pupils under him, my good friend Geoff Huff and myself were not the best at aerobatics but prided our selves on our low flying prowess.

Rogers didn't believe in navigation and often watched us in the flight office in puzzled amusement drawing lines on maps allowing for drift by angling and striking off wind direction and speed and arriving at a second line giving us our (theoretical) heading and ETA. His method, and he had flown successfully all over the USA, was to fly over the airfield on approx. course, pick up the first pinpoint and E-A-S-E it back on course and by the time the third fix came up he was dead on the right heading and this he demonstrated regularly.

As an example, one day we had to fly a two hour navigational exercise "dog legging" over three towns in Texas and then back to base with myself piloting and my instructor sitting in the back seat as a mute observer. We had our usual met. briefing and were told there was a strong 15 knot wind from due East, and laid our courses out on the charts accordingly, Rogers watching with his usual cynical smile.

We were the last plane to take-off, came over the centre of the airfield and headed for the first pinpoint on the ground. Finding this too much to the left, I was in a quandary, whether to follow RAF procedure and charts and possibly upset my instructor or e-a-s-e it back on track, I decided on the latter. By the time the course had been corrected three times as per the landmarks, all the rest of the flight had disappeared, possibly some 30 degrees to the right. I was thinking "I've made a real mess up of this and its too late now to chase after them", when a clearly delighted Rogers couldn't contain himself any longer, broke silence and in between gusts of laughter said, " I shouldn't tell you this but we're the only b-------s on track". We were the first plane back to base, the others getting completely lost, we were told that there had been a 180 degree change in wind direction by the time we took off, the 15 knot East wind veering to West.

Rogers was delighted that once again his navigational expertise had prevailed. Perhaps he should have been employed as Nav adviser to the RAF or better still the US Air force who occasionally were known to stray off course (sometimes complete squadrons!). What ever he did in fog or cloud down to the ground I never ascertained or asked about (I still have sleepless nights puzzling about that). Our DALTON calculator/computer we had strapped to our left leg used to frighten the daylights out of him.

One Saturday morning having cut swathes across wheat fields with our wing tips, circled odd farmhouses in near vertical banks until various attractive lady friends would wave some personal item of apparel from a window when we came up over a hedge and spotted a huge transporter covered with coloured lights on a remote highway doing 60 to 70 mph. He brought the Stearman down behind this truck, matched the speed, virtually trundled the wheels across the top, bucketing in the turbulence, then, when level with the cabin, came down until the wheels appeared in front of the windscreen, pulled up, stood on our tail so that they couldn't get our number and I remember looking back and seeing about five people side by side (presumably driver, co-driver, observer and two navigators) with horrified faces, the driver fighting with the wheel and the truck snaking from one side to the other (in those days there was only one car every ten minutes on these roads). I don't think many pilots would be capable of carrying out this manoeuvre and even less would have attempted it.

When I was on advanced flying on Harvards, I ran into Rogers in the flight room and told him the Harvard was even better than the Stearman at low flying, he couldn't believe it until I said it had retractable undercarriage and you could fly 3 feet lower, at which he doubled up with laughter.

He did have a wonderful sense of humour, one day as I brought our Stearman in to land on the grass and across the runway with gusting side winds, the Stearman directly in front of us ground looped (as was their wont) and my instructor, choking with laughter announced "That's your Group Captain and I bet his a-r-s-e is red"! When we had to make a cross country flight and overnight stay at Wichita or somewhere, being young I asked what the night life was like, he replied sadly, "At 9 o/c they w-i-n-d the sidewalks in".

The Americans often have this simple but devastatingly humorous retort and I am reminded of a Texas reunion at the Café Royal in London when someone publicly asked if anyone knew the whereabouts of a certain instructor and another instructor announced, "The last time I heard about him, he was dead".

I think we all have moments that stay in the mind as if it was yesterday and we will never forget. It's when one starts remembering things that never happened that one needs to worry!

Ah! Memories.

MY STORY

By Mostyn Rowland.

Like most young men of my age group (I was then 18 years old) who joined the RAF to fly I volunteered as an Observer and after passing out on Oral, Written, and Medical Exams during a couple of days at Western-Super-Mare was called up in July 1941. Most of us went to ACRC in London then onto ITW at Stratford upon Avon and then in Dec.1941 I was posted to No.4 AOS West Freugh Nr Stranraer in Scotland

Mostyn Rowland Second from Right

I passed out in June 1942 and was proud to wear the O brevet. Then still staying in Scotland and posted to 19 OTU Kinloss for crew training we did a one day trip with a Staff Pilot in an Anson. On the night of 17/6/42 we took off at 23.50 hrs with another Staff Pilot and another Anson. Looking back, I think it was a mistake to send us off for it was raining and steadily got worse. We did the exercise to the best of our ability but when the Staff Pilot tried to land, visibility was so bad we couldn't get down. He tried a couple of times but after seeing mountains on each side of us he eventually gave it up as a bad job and headed for the North Sea coast where he gave the order to bale out.

You can imagine how we felt but thought it better than crashing and of course we were getting low on fuel after 4.40 hrs flying. I jumped and did manage to pull the rip cord when clear of the tail plane and I must say it is a wonderful feeling when the parachute actually opens and you are drifting down. It still being dark, I hit the ground on a mountain and injured my ankle on landing. I managed to crawl and hop until I found a farmhouse where the farmer came out with a shot-gun, he of course couldn't tell the difference between a Welsh and German accent. He was persuaded who I was and managed to get help and after the others were rounded up we were flown back from Dyce aerodrome near Aberdeen to Kinloss.

I was in the sick bay at Kinloss for a day or two before being transferred to Raigmore Hospital in Inverness for x-ray's and tests. After a few weeks I was allowed to go out into the town in Hospital Blue until I was fit enough to travel back to Kinloss. They were satisfied with my progress and sent me down to a recuperation centre in Blackpool.

My billet there was a guest house on the South shore where we were expected to help with the household chores such as potato bashing, of course we had to go to a Centre for exercises and such but had quite a bit of time to enjoy Blackpool.

The month passed quickly and at the end of it found myself back at Kinloss.

After three more x-country's' in Ansons' we crewed up to go on Whitleys'. The first three day trips, our Sgt Pilot had a Staff Pilot with him and after doing a short flight on our own, we were briefed to do a fairly long x-country the following day. We were flying down the West coast of Scotland to the Isle of Man, it being a lovely day, the pilot suggested I take over for a short while. This I did and enjoyed it, but after about ten minutes one engine suddenly packed up. I was out of the seat and the pilot back in at no time at all, but no sooner done than the other engine packed in. He could only presume that there was some kind of fuel fault and after losing height decided it was time to ditch. The rest of us went back to near the door to await a landing which turned out to be quite good. We got the dinghy out through the door, inflated it and all got in safe and sound with the pilot climbing out through the top hatch and walking along the top of the plane.

We were congratulating ourselves on our escape and by this time the plane was sinking quite fast and we were still attached to it. We could not at first find the knife to cut the rope free of the plane but like the sprog crew we were one of us was sitting on it. However we did manage it before the plane sank below the water.

Another example of inexperience was when the pilot fired the Very pistol into the wind and the flare just managed to miss us. However we were only a few miles out from the Scottish coast and an Air Sea Rescue launch came out from Stranraer and picked us up. We were taken back to my old training airfield at West Freugh from where we were taken back to Kinloss. We never did see our pilot after this and could only presume he was taken off flying duties.

Our luck then changed for the better when we crewed up with a Canadian F/Lt. pilot who had been instructing in Canada. We finished off our day and night x-countries together and after spending a few days at a staging post at Abingdon found ourselves posted to St .Eval in Cornwall. This was to carry out Anti-Submarine patrols in the Bay of Biscay on Whitleys' where the procedure was to do 8-9-10hours patrol one day followed by a rest day and then an air test to get ready for another patrol.

The weather was usually poor being in December 1942 and our only navigation aid was mostly to take drifts on the white caps. This one day was particularly bad and returning back we reached land not knowing if it was England, France or Ireland. It was Southern Ireland and we quickly broke radio silence and got a QDM back to base though when we hit the English coast we were so short of fuel we were forced to land at Chivenor, North of St. Eval.

On another patrol we did attack a U-boat but our depth charges hung up and although we did a square search we didn't have another chance. On one of our rest days we went into Newquay, had a fairly good time and got to bed about 12 o'clock. The next thing we knew was being woken up about 4 o'clock, a crew had been taken ill and we were to replace them taking off about 6am. You may imagine how we felt after being out the night before. However we got back safely and then after we had done about 8 patrols went back to Abingdon to await a posting on to 4 engine bombers.

That of course is another story, but we did live to tell it.

617 SQUADRON

Terry Kearns

A few years ago our branch visited the D-Day museum on Southsea sea front. Jim Bevis and myself had got behind the main Party and were studying the tapestries when we were joined by the late Terry Kearns DSO. DFC .DFM. our one time chairman, a New Zealander from 617 etc .etc.. After some time he casually mentioned his involvement in D. Day and eventually told us that in his opinion the Dieppe raid was not such a disaster as it had been painted and that the truth might one day come out, and that as a result we managed to obtain some of the latest radar from Pourville near Dieppe. It was set up on a headland in UK and for months 'selected' Lancaster crews experimented with different lengths of aluminium foil (Window) till in the end they had the operators of the German radar guessing as to whether the bay was full of different sized ships or Lancaster's in the air above.

On D Day the vast armada set off in the direction of Calais, half way across veered towards Normandy and sixteen Lancaster's from 617 squadron continued towards the Calais area flying rectangular orbits dropping window at a forward speed of eight knots - the Operation was known as 'Taxable', completely fooling the German radar observers who's scopes showed a Channel and bay full of ships, their binoculars, nothing. I made the remark that we should have had one chap rowing in and giving a two finger salute (as per Capt. Bligh) but that I do not think 'they' would have thought it funny, and blasted him off the earth with thousands of frustrated shells!. This is how I remember him telling this story. I obviously did not take it down at the time as I never expected to be writing this account.

YEAR: 1944	AIRCRAFT		PILOT, OR 1st PILOT.	2ND PILOT, PUPIL, OR PASSENGER.	DUTY (INCLUDING RESULTS AND REMARKS)
MONTH DATE	Type	No.			TOTALS BROUGHT FORWARD
APRIL 7	MOSQUITO	976	SELF	F/O BARCLAY	BOMBING WAINFLEET & X-COUNTRY
" 18	"	976	SELF	F/O BARCLAY	DIVE BOMBING VAINCOURT
" 19	"	976	SELF	F/O BARCLAY	77TH OPERATION RAILWAY SIDINGS JUVISY BACKER - 2 x 500 x 4 x 500 - bombed
" 20	"	976	SELF	F/O BARCLAY	78TH OPERATION RAILWAY MARSHALLING YARD LA CHAPELLE N/PARIS - V.G. RAID - BOMBED
" 22	"	976	SELF	F/O BARCLAY	79TH OPERATION - BRUNSWICK - 4 SPOTS - RAID DOUBTFUL - SPOTS LAID ON BASE
" 24	"	976	SELF	F/O BARCLAY	1ST MANSTON
" 24	"	976	SELF	F/O BARCLAY	80TH OPERATION - MUNICH - 4 SPOTS ON GFF - EXCELLENT RAID - RETURNED 2700 LBS FUEL IN EA.
" 25	"	176	SELF	F/O BARCLAY	MANSTON TO BASE
" 27	LANCASTER	ME146	SELF	CREW	FROM BENBROKE DOWN
				SUMMARY FOR APRIL 1944	
				UNIT: 627 SQDN	AIRCRAFT 1. LANCASTER
				DATE: 29TH MAY 1944	TYPES 2. MOSQUITO
				SIGNATURE	3.
MAY 3rd	MOSQUITO		SELF	F/O BARCLAY	81ST OPERATION TO MILITARY BARRACKS AT MAILLEY - 4 SPOTS - BOMBED V.GOOD
" 7	MOSQUITO		SELF	F/L CASHMORE	TESTING & A/C VANFLEET
" 8	LANCASTER	KM972	SELF		GEE HOMINGS & TACTICS
" 9	"	ME558	SELF	CREW	GEE HOMINGS & TACTICS
" 10	"	657	SELF	CREW	GEE HOMINGS & TACTICS

GRAND TOTAL [Cols. (1) to (10)]
11.35 Hrs. 40 Mins.

TOTALS CARRIED FORWARD

	SINGLE-ENGINE AIRCRAFT		MULTI-ENGINE AIRCRAFT	
	DAY	NIGHT	DAY	NIGHT
	DUAL	PILOT	DUAL	PILOT
	22.35	26.25		
	22.35	26.25		

YEAR 1944		AIRCRAFT		PILOT, OR 1st PILOT	2nd PILOT, PUPIL, OR PASSENGER	DUTY (Including Results and Remarks)	SINGLE-ENGINE AIRCRAFT			
							DAY		NIGHT	
MONTH	DATE	Type	No.				DUAL	PILOT	DUAL	PILOT
						TOTALS BROUGHT FORWARD	22.35	46.25		
JUNE	3	LANCASTER	LM 497	SELF	CREW F/O BARTLETT F/O PATRICK F/O TOTTEN	x—Country Jamica Ballarnogar Saverhouse				
"	5	"	ML 557	SELF	F/O STEWART F/O LUMAS F/O HUNT Sgt METCHIN P/O KAGAN P/O BUCKLEY	82 no OPERATION — TACTICAL OPERATION. CAUSING A DIVERSION TO COVER THE INITIAL LANDINGS ON THE CHERBOURG PENINSULA HT 3000'— BELIEVE VERY SUCCESSFUL				
"	8	"	DV 146	SELF	F/O PETCH F/O BARTLETT F/O PATRICK F/O TOTTEN F/O STEWART W/O BUCKLEY F/O PETCH	83 A OPERATION TO SAUMUR TUNNEL BOMBING VERY ACCURATE LAND 1 x 12000 lb. TALLBOY — BIRGE HITS: TUNNEL L MOUTH Believed Very Successfull R/O				
"	13	"	ME 559	SELF	CREW F/O PETCH F/O TOTTEN F/O HENDERSON	H/S JAM/FEET 84th OPERATION to SUBMARINE PENS at BREST R/O SIGHTED				
"	14	"	DV 146	SELF	F/O PARKER F/O BUCKLEY F/O PETCH	81 Le HAVRE — Formation Bombing Napors F/P SQDN. ON FIRST — No E/A SIGHTED				
"	15	"	DV 246	SELF	F/O TATE F/O TOTTEN F/O HENDERSON F/O FULFORD F/O BUCKLEY	85th OPERATION TO E BOAT Pens AT BOULOGNE - FORMATION - FIGHTER ESCORT CLOUD OVER TARGET. TIE/TARGET CANADIAN				
"	20	"	JB 139	SELF	F/O PETCH F/O HENDERSON Sgt TATE F/O SEACLAY F/O ELSWOOD F/O BUCKLEY Sgt METCHIN	By Dingle OP.G — Pas De Calais Area 86 TH SPECIAL TARGET. LOADED 4x 4000. LOW 1st WAVE — EXCELLENT RESULT CLOUD OVER TARGET — RETURNED WITH LOAD.				
						TOTALS CARRIED FORWARD	99 35 56.25			

GRAND TOTAL [Cols. (1) to (10)] 18 36 Hrs. 7 Mins.

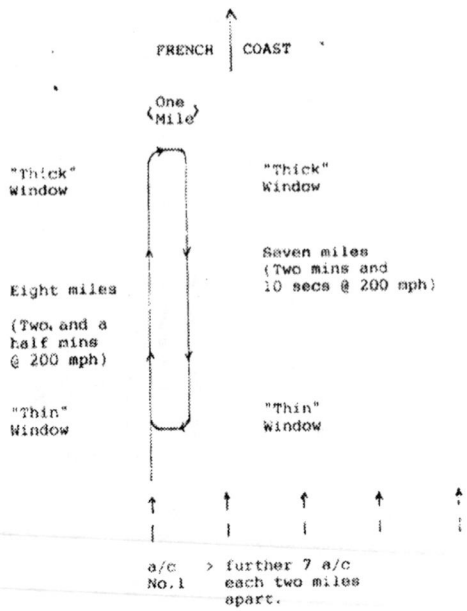

Operation Taxable required 16 Lancasters of 617 Sqn flying precise circuits.

On another occasion we asked him how many Op.'s he had done and he said "Oh, I don't know, a few". We eventually dragged it out of him that it was 90, We asked him how he had managed to survive so many Op.'s, some as a Pathfinder, and he said 'a bit of luck'. He then told us that his crew, from the moment they were airborne, would report non-stop on the slightest detail on anything they saw around them such as 'Observer to Skipper there's a light on the ground at 3 o'clock travelling to 9 o'clock, could be a motor cycle ?. and then, from say, the rear gunner, "Yes, I think you're right", each crew member vying with each other to see something first, so when the message came through on the intercom "Skipper, bandit, corkscrew", as Terry pushed the stick forward, tracers shot over the cockpit. How much of this quick reaction was due to "a bit of luck" and how much to "Could be a motor-cycle skipper"

The D day landing on June 5th was his 82nd Op. and on the 8th he dropped a 'Tallboy' earthquake bomb scoring a direct hit on the Saumur tunnel preventing German Tank reinforcements from reaching the fighting in Normandy. In the process he obliterated Leonard Cheshire's marking flare preventing the Lancs from seeing the target. Cheshire remarked "Hold on chaps I will have to mark again". On the 14th and (his 84th Op.) he was back at Le Havre bombing the U-Boat pens; on the 15th E-Boat pens at Boulogne and on the 20th (86th Op) special target Pas de Calais area.

Quite an interesting and busy June, as he might well have said!.
By Rex Hurley from Official Records and Family.

RAF EXPERIENCES 1940-46.

By Joe Smeaton.

March 1940, Shortly before my 19th birthday I went to Romford Aircrew recruiting centre to volunteer and after satisfying the M.O. that I was fit, was sent home to await instructions.

In early June I was Ordered to report to RAF Uxbridge where I had a full aircrew medical and passed. In common with 99% of the recruits I put in for pilot training with wireless operator/air gunner as second choice, my advanced maths being shaky. We were sworn in and given our service numbers (932081) and it still has not come up in the lottery!.

I received call up for 10th Oct.1940 and reported to RAF Blackpool for Morse training up to 12 words per minute. The RAF used the top story of Burtons the Tailors as our training room and we also learnt how to march, using the length of the promenade as a parade ground. During a very heavy gale we had to break ranks to hold on to the beach rails, dodging a capsized tram in the process!.

Having passed OK we were sent to RAF Cranwell in Jan. 41 for advanced Morse and wireless theory and then our introduction to flying. Firstly in a de-Havilland to see if we were air sick or panic stricken and then for more Morse training, air to ground transmitting and receiving, this taking place in a Vickers Valentia aircraft piloted by a Czech pilot, eight of us wireless trainees and one instructor were passengers. The aircraft had been used for flying in mountainous parts in India and was thought to be reliable, however, the engines cut-out soon after take- off and we crashed nose first gracefully into a tall tree near Saxilby in Lincolnshire. Luckily no one was badly injured and we all made a sliding fall through the leaves and branches to the ground, some 20ft below, but the plane was a write off!. After a few more 'radio' flights we concentrated on wireless theory and finished the course in April.

I was sent to Pembroke Dock to spend two weeks on a radio station in the middle of Milford Haven and was then posted to Jurby, Isle of Man for my three weeks gunnery course, flying in Blenheims by Polish pilots, just to test our nerves!. At the end of the course we were awarded our Sergeants Stripes and Wireless/Ops badge with our coveted air gunners half wing on our chest.

I was then posted to Cottismore near Oakham in Rutland, training on Ansons at first and then was introduced to Hampdens. There was not very much room for the four man crew, the pilots were fond of the Aircraft once they had become used to them. The navigator who also carried out the duties of bomb aimer, had to leave his seat in order to crawl full length into the nose to aim and drop the bombs on to the target - hopefully.

Wing Commander Learoyd VC and Flight Sergeant Hannah VC were both instructors at Cottismore and on passing out I was posted to their old Squadrons (49 & 83) at Scampton near Lincoln on the 4th Oct 41.

I joined the crew of F.O.Cumming as rear gunner and reserve W/Op and should explain the layout of the crew. The navigator was seated immediately behind the pilot at a small table above which was an astro-dome and plotted courses for the pilot. But when near the target, crawled into the front bombing position from where he released the bomb load on to the target, and immediately gave the pilot the course for home.

While this was happening, the upper wireless operator and rear gunners would be alert with their cupolas open and Vickers guns cocked and ready with one drum of 303 bullets on each. The under gunner with his gun similarly arranged in a semi- prone position, both gunners being able to fire at will on an identified enemy aircraft within range and also keep the pilot informed of any 'flak' getting too close.

My first operation with 83 Squadron was on 12.10.41, one year and ten days from when I joined up. F.O.Cumming was the pilot, Sgt. Alec Urquhart the navigator, Sgt Cox the Wop/A.G. and myself as rear gunner. The target that night was Bremen - my first baptism of fire, but nothing hit us in spite of being caught in a cone of searchlights for what seemed an uncomfortably long time before our bombs were dropped on target and the navigator gleefully gave the course for home. Half way across the North Sea we received radio orders to land at RAF Finningly because Scampton was covered with thick fog. On landing the first person I met was a friend, Ron Jessop, who had been in the same form as me at East Ham Grammar School. He had been on the same Op. that night, was a pilot and came through the war unscathed and was awarded the D.F.M. So many planes landed at Finningly that night that no beds were available so we slept on a snooker table in the Sgts. Mess with all the usual remarks about balls in the pockets! Our next operation was on Kiel, on 1st Nov.41 was successful, but 8.05 hours was a long cold trip. From then until 20.1 42 we attacked Essen, Cologne twice, Brest (U.Boat pens etc.), Dusseldorf, Soestberg airfield, Bordeaux (dropping mines in the Gironde), Leewarden and Munster.

On the 21.1.42 we were transferred to 49 Sqd. as we were half way through our tour and 83 Sqd. was converting to Manchesters and Lancasters, we took our Hampdens with us. By this time I was 1st WOP/AG because Sgt. Cox had been transferred to the Flight Commanders Crew and I took over his position and a near friend Sgt. Ian Smith joining us as 2nd WOP/AG. In passing I should mention what a delightful character Sgt.Cox was who amongst other things used to recite the Gettysberg address in full whilst standing on the crew room table and subsequently christened the 'General'.

Our first trip with the new squadron was mine laying in the Sea off Ferscheling, satisfying but not exciting followed by the day-light attack on the German battleships Scharnhorst and Gneisenau which were making a dash up the Channel. Unfortunately fog was thick right down to the waves and we missed them, we did attack a destroyer through a gap in the fog, but doubt if we hit it. Sadly the 'General' (Sgt. Cox and crew were lost on this unfortunate mission).

Our other operations with 49 Sqd. were bombing Wilhelmshaven and Essen then mine laying off the Ameland and the Frisians, Lorient twice and Bordeaux, then low level bombing of Lubeck on 28.3.42, we answered heavy small arms fire with our own brand, all along the main road to the docks. Next trip was attacking NW German railway communications, a 7hr. trip, Cologne, Hamburg, Essen three times. Returning from Essen 12.4.42 we were attacked by a JU 88 firing a rear mounted cannon and guns from below us as we crossed the Zuider Zee. We started to lose height and power and the pilot ordered me to send an SOS so that we could be tracked as we crossed the North Sea. As I touched the Morse key the top fell off, a bullet had gone through the hinge, I was able to bend some wire loosely round it and managed to send the message. I also found that a bullet had hit the transmitter but luckily it was still working. As we were about half way home the pilot ordered me to cancel the SOS but to ask for priority landing permission which was granted and we landed safely back at base.

The Cannon shell had gone through the port wing without touching the fuel tank and when we reported this to the gunnery leader, he said we must have been asleep as the JU88 did not have a rear firing cannon. Our protests were not accepted but fortunately about two weeks later a picture was published in 'Flight Magazine' with the caption "Rear firing cannon now fitted to the JU88!". The under gunner Ian Smith and myself went to the Flight Commanders office and pointed out that our report had been correct and he accepted our version. I suspect the gunnery leader was duly informed, we did not bother to ask him! but we did leave a copy of Flight on his desk open at the informing page!.

I finished my tour on 14th May.42 with a trip to Dortmund and for the next 3 months I was on operational training on Manchesters and Lancasters until someone realised I had just finished my first tour in August 42. I was posted as a WOP/instructor to Hampstead Norris a satellite of Harwell operational training unit on Wellingtons. During this time the first 1,000 bomber raid took place and every available aircraft was ordered to take part, including all the Wellingtons at Hampstead Norris and I was expected to go. However the Flt.Lt. in charge of the Wireless/Op .Instructors had not been on operations and decided he would go instead of me as I was the last Wop/AG to have finished his tour. It may have been my last flight as Flt.Lt. Jock Clark and the crew were shot down over Cologne and none survived, so I was lucky, although any alterations of the crew and timing may have a different sequence of events..

Shortly afterwards at the end of May 43 I was posted to RAF Wigtown, a few miles from Stranraer in Scotland, again as staff Wop/Ag instructor flying in Ansons (530 hours) until May 44. My pilot there was Pete Souster, a good friend and pilot, so when I was posted to O.T.U. at Barford St.John, I volunteered to go as his W/Op or Signaller as we were now called. By this time I was a Warrant Officer and four W/Op. friends and their pilots were posted with us to O.T.U.

After further training on Stirlings at Chedburgh in Suffolk on Lancasters at Feltwell we were posted to go to a Sqn. at Tuddenham to commence our tour on Lancasters. The big difference now was that most operations were in daylight and in loose formation with the rest of the squadron. So my second tour of operations started on 16th Dec.44 to bomb Siegen, so much more comfortable than the Hampden and heating made it unnecessary to be heavily clad although the rear and mid upper gunners needed to be more cosily dressed especially on the few night operations. The pressure was really on the Germans now, our programme for the rest of December was Trier on the 23rd, short break for Christmas, then Rheydt on the 27th, Cologne 28th and a Happy New Year to Vohwinkel on the 31st, all hotly contested by the 'Jerry's' but the weight of our numbers must have left them gasping. On the 2nd Jan.45 we reverted to a night attack on Nuremberg with a maximum show of strength giving a new meaning to the Nuremberg 'rally'. On the 5th Jan. attacked Ludwigshafen in daylight and ran into heavy flak and returned on 3 engines, then on the 7th Jan another long trip to Munich (8 hours). We slightly strayed over the Swiss border on the way back and they very correctly fired on us to confirm their neutrality, missing us to be sporty, no doubt! Three more trips in Jan. took us to Saarbruken and Ernwick by day and Wann-Eikel by night. The return from Saarbruken was a bit of a menace as thick fog covered most of England and we flew along the South coast at low level until we found a clear patch at Predannack in Cornwall and managed to land there.

From 7th of Feb.to the 10th we were sent to Feltwell for a G.H. course and exercise, this being the latest radar aid for finding exactly where you were or near enough if it wasn't being jammed too much. The rest of Feb. took us to Wesel, Buer, Dortmund, and Helsenkirchen twice by day and Dortmund by night, all successful but still contested fiercely by Jerry. The 1st, 2nd, 4th & 5th of March read Kamen. Cologne, Wann-Eikel and Gelsenkirchen in daylight, 6th March Wesel at night, then 11th, 12th, 21st and 29th Essen, Munster and Hallendorf (Brunswicj) by day. This was my 25th operation on Lancasters and completed my second tour of operations, the rest of the crew had 5 more trips to do to complete their first tour. I was sorry to leave the crew and asked to carry on with them but apparently an enthusiastic young officer was anxious to get five operations under his belt before Jerry folded up, so I had to say goodbye to Peter Souster pilot, Dennis Warren navigator, Lance Butcher bomb aimer, Reg Ware flight engineer, Taff Taylor mid upper and Frank Tickle rear gunner, although we had one reunion in London in 47. I met Taff by chance in the 60's and I heard he had died some five years after, he was 44 when we flew on operations and was the fittest man in the crew, could do about 50 'pull ups' on the bars while the rest of us dropped out at about ten!. Peter Souster kept in touch while he was flying for B.E.A. and he arranged to be pilot on a holiday trip to Paris that we were taking. Half way across he ordered drinks for us and having handed over to the 2nd pilot, came and gravely saluted us as if we were important passengers. I could not help remembering the time I'd put him to bed after a heavy night in the mess bar at Wigtown.

I was awarded the D.F.C. and posted to Lynham and awaited demob, while flashing Aldis lamps to landing aircraft from a caravan at the end of the runway. All of them landed safely despite my lack of practice.

The Germans by this time had two new model fighters but the RAF & USAF had the weight of numbers to overwhelm them, nevertheless out of 7 pairs of W/Ops from Wigtown who were posted to 90 squadron, only 3 pairs survived. My good friends Les Page from Haywards Heath, Joe Edwards from London and Dutch Holland were killed in the last weeks of the war. My friend and navigator from Hampden days, Alec Urquart joined 617 Squadron and was killed on the Dambusters Raid.

Peter Souster after serving with B.E.A., flew for various Middle East Airlines and we lost touch over the years. My cousin Sgt Bob Smeaton trained at Blackpool, at the same time as me, was killed when his plane crashed into a Welsh mountains while training.

Lancaster

We remember all these friends particularly at the impressive annual service held at Runnymeade Memorial for 55.000 aircrew who lost their lives flying with Bomber Command 1939-45. We also remembered Air Marshall 'Butch' Harris at the unveiling of the memorial to him at St.Clement Danes church, without his dogged determination the history of Bomber Command would not have been so successful!.

A DAYS WORK

Ken Trott.

On April 29th I was stationed at Needs Oar Point airfield near Beaulieu with 197 Squadron- 146 Wing Tactical Air Force, when we were first called at 4.30am. At that time we were under canvas and breakfast was taken before reporting to the briefing tent. 197 Squadron was an operational Hawker Typhoon fighter Bomber squadron and we were given our first mission of the day as a Ramrod over France but the weather was bad inland and we turned back which resulted in our bombs being dropped on a secondary target. We returned from France about 7a.m. and were told to remain on standby -this resulted in a second breakfast! about 7.45a.m.. The wing again formed up for a formation flight to Harrowbear Airfield north of Plymouth. Upon arrival we were told to go to the Mess for breakfast which was still being served and then report for briefing, as young men our appetite was enormous!.

JP648 196 Sqn. Sept. 1943, F/O K. A. J. Trott.

Later in the morning we were told that our target was Morlais in the Brest Peninsula. It seemed that a number of vessels were moored in that area. I was the Wings CO's number 2 and we took off and flew low level before sighting the French coast, at which point the Wing climbed to 12,000ft, proceeded inland and then turned for our attack on the ships and the quickest way home. We then made a dive bombing attack on the ships which were moored below, before pulling out at about 1,500ft doing about 550 knots and using our 20mm cannon on the way down. I recorded in my log book of seeing one direct hit and two near misses, the rest of the Wing followed and we then formed up for a low level flight in battle formation for our return journey to England.

No aircraft were lost although there had been plenty of light flack and also balloons to cope with. Back at Harrowbear we were told to remain on standby. However no further orders came through and we returned to Needs Oar Point the following morning. Total flying time involved 3 hours 39 minutes, plus one hour return to base.

TOO CLOSE !

By Ken Trott.

In July 1944 I was stationed at Hurn Airfield having moved with 197 Squadron (Hawker Typhoons) from Needs Oar Point near Beaulieu, our base for the D Day operations. At that time we were carrying out offensive operations over France in support of the troops now based in Normandy.

On the 11th July we flew from Hurn to make our first landing on French soil at airfield B.3., St.Croix. This had been constructed with metal tracking to provide a base for refuelling and tented accommodation. On the 11th and 12th we carried out operations over France, the plan being to stay there until the evening of the 13th July when we would then return to Hurn. Later that day four of us were briefed for an armed reconnaissance in the Caen area, the section being led by Wing Co. Baldwin, his No.2, myself and my No.2. We took off about 5p.m. and headed in the direction of Caen, while in the area south of Le Havre I spotted a German half track troop carrier and requested permission to attack, this was given and the two of us turned and made a cannon attack, on the way down, on pulling away I queried if we could make another attack as the vehicle had now been abandoned, however I was informed by the Wing Co. to rejoin him as there were 30 plus ME 109's attacking.

I quickly climbed up to approx. 4,000ft and spotted several 109's ahead of me just below broken cloud, I closed to make an attack but they had obviously seen us and broke to sweep past and out of sight. By this time I was in cloud and on my own, As I came out of cloud I noticed a solitary ME 109 coming towards me, I lined up for a head on attack firing my cannon, The next minute I realised I would have to break to avoid a collision, as I did so my starboard wing collided with the wing of the 109 and I felt my head hit the cockpit cover and my left shoulder the side of the cockpit, My helmet, oxygen mask, goggles and revolver holster were torn from my body and I hurtled into space, with only my parachute intact, I realised I would have to pull the ripcord as my altitude was only about 3,000ft. The next minute the canopy opened and I lost consciousness.

I came round to find myself hanging from a tree in an orchard surrounded by several armed Germans, one of whom was attempting to release me from the parachute harness, this he did and I fell on top of him to the ground where I lay for a while. A German motioned me to get up and put my arms up, it was then that I found my left arm remained by my side, I couldn't move it in any way. We then proceeded across some fields to a French farm house, which appeared to be the local German H.Q.

I was taken up some stairs and met a German officer seated behind a desk. I saluted him, a wise move as I was then invited to sit down. After a brief interrogation I was asked if I felt well enough to be moved, I nodded and was then escorted to an open top car parked in the farm yard. We set off with me and my escort on the back seat and after a few minutes arrived in the village of Pont Le Eveque where I was taken to a school room. By that time I was feeling rather unwell and coughing up blood. The guard called his superior and eventually I was moved to a nearby hospital.

Over the next few weeks I was moved to a hospital in Paris, then on to Trier in Luxembourg and finally arrived at Stalag Luft 111, Sagan on the 30th August, where I was admitted to the camp hospital and stayed until early October before entering the East camp British compound, where I stayed until moved again, due to the Russian advance, to Nuremberg then finally to Moosburg near Munchen, where I was liberated by the American Army in April 1945.

FRENCH MEETING

By K.Trott.

In 1990 Ken Trott and his wife Kay were visiting the area in France, Pont-L'Eveque where he crashed on 13th July 1944. He was with 197 Squadron flying out of Hurn. They had called at the Town Hall to see Monsieur le Maire, but he was not there that day and were talking to a Daniel Bonamy who when told that Ken was an RAF pilot, related an incident he had seen from his back door. According to his report " An ME109 and a Typhoon were swirling around in their flight. Suddenly they collided and the German plane cut the Typhoon's right wing off whose pilot ejected. I saw him come down in his parachute and fell, I could not see where". He presumed that he had been killed. At that point Ken pointed to himself and said "It was me" and Daniel Bonamy says, "we fell in each others arms".

Back in England Ken wrote to Daniel Bonamy regarding this episode and asking if any of his friends had also witnessed the accident and his parachute descent and if anyone knew what happened to the other plane. When he was captured he was taken to a college classroom where he wrote on the blackboard his name rank and number and remembers there were two French students in the room and wondered if any one remembers. Someone did.

Ken Trott, entouré de ses amis Français de Saint-Martin-aux-Chartrains, exhibe le petit morceau de on avion

A Gustave Breavoine related his meeting with the Englishman - quote "But I know where it took place, that evening I was in the neighbouring pasture helping my father with hay making. When the fight started we got as far as covering the straw in case of rain". Gustave remembers the end of the combat "The Englishman fell next door to Augar the cooper of Saint-Martin, the father in law of Henri Leon the former Barber. The plane burst into flames, the ammunition was exploding. The Germans came immediately on the scene and the pilot was taken prisoner". As for the German pilot who was quite elderly and had been brought back from the Russian front because of the Normandy invasion, he fell on his face without hurting himself after gliding down and force landing.

A little later Ken returned to France and was taken to the meadow at Saint-Martin aux Chartrains where he fell and was presented with a little piece of his plane. It was a time of deep emotion for him. "I shall put this in my wallet, it will never leave my pocket" he said.

Footnote: Gustave was only a youngster at the time of helping with the hay making. He refers to the German pilot as being quite elderly and probably thought that Ken was a rather ancient Englishman, he must have been 21-22 at the time! Editor.

THE BEIRA PATROL

Douglas Cook

The Beira Patrol was set up, under the auspices of a United Nations resolution following the Rhodesian 1965 unilateral declaration of independence. It was to enforce the trade embargo specifically to stop oil imports to Rhodesia through the Mosambique port of Beira by air surveillance and ship patrol. A small RAF detachment was placed at Majunga operating Shackletons but by 1970 people were saying that the tankers were mammoth, they were sailing round the Horn, the vessels were too big to enter the port of Beira, that the pipeline from there to Rhodesia was out of order and anyway they had adequate supplies from neighbouring African States. The UK was unfortunately politically committed to continue!. The Nimrod was by now rapidly replacing the Shackleton and the MoD was reluctant to commit the new A/C to the Majunga task. Then the decommissioning date of the last RN aircraft carriers was some years before the AEW version of the Nimrod could be ready to fill the gap left by the loss of the large RN AEW Gannet at sea. The answer was to run on one sqn of Shackletons, both to continue with the Majunga task in the short term and then for them to be fitted with the Gannet's radar to provide an interim AEW capability. This all required some complicated planning, and that is what I was doing when in 1970 I was chosen to be the next CO at Majunga. After a French language refresher course I was promoted and posted to Madagascar as Le Commandant du Detachement de la Royal Air Force a Majunga.

The detachment had to be seen to be non permanent. This meant tents or rented accommodation where possible, resulting in the Tech Site and Comms being in a site near the airport, and airmen billeted in watchman's buildings from an earlier road building project, with barrack, mess and bar facilities, first aid centre. This was Camp Britanique. Senior NCO's were housed in an ex maternity hospital. HQ admin staff were in two flats above H.Q. office in a shop in the main Street of Majunga!, whilst Engineering and Supply offices rented a bungalow outside town. The C.O. had a house in town and Aircrew officers a first floor flat as their mess. Being 16 degrees South of the Equator we had two seasons, wet and dry and always hot which was trying on man and machines. It is a tribute to the training, dedication and professionalism of all the RAF personnel who made up the Detachment over nearly seven years that the operational task was always completed. We returned to UK in 1972 and left behind many friends and the place where the trustworthy old Shackleton completed 20 years of maritime patrols.

The reality was that Majunga Airport consisted of one runway and a small Aircraft Servicing Pan with an extra bit of concrete laid for the Shackletons but every thing else, in theory, had to be taken away at the end of the detachments life in line with an agreement between the Governments of UK and Malagasy. The Tech site was in tents and aluminium prefab huts (Altents) and latterly an inflatable air-conditioned store for the electric spares, all tactically disposed under mango, breadfruit and kapok trees, hence kapok fluff in everything.

We flew patrols randomly, if an aircraft was unserviceable it flew the next day. One day our last engine refused to start. I remembered we had sticking commutators in the past at St Eval and I knew the cure, so I instructed the young electrician to belt the starter with a piece of 4x2 and a large hammer. To humour me and to carry out orders he did and on the third blow, hey presto, it worked! (I heard later his mates gave him hell for having to get the Wing Commanders advice). Most Shackleton hangers have a hole in the floor called a radar pit to save having to jack the Aircraft up 10 ft in the case of scanner hydraulic problems. We dug a simple hole in the rock hard ground of the air servicing pan near the Technical site and when not in use, covered it with pegged down steel sheets and ground markers. The DOE inspector dutifully turned a blind eye to this unofficial hole!.

Our supplies and shopping lists were ordered by hand speed Morse (a dying art at that time) hence on one occasion twelve Shackleton tail wheel steering arms for ground steering arrived (we only had two Shackletons) instead of stainless steel bolts, the code number being one digit out.

When the Detachment left Majunga and returned to the UK in 1972 it left behind many friends and the place where the Shackleton completed its last maritime patrol tasks of its first 21 years in operational service. The AEW role was to add another 19 years to that.... but that is another story.

FLIGHTS BY THE FORGOTTEN

By Ellis Bedford, WOM/AG,
Nos. 240, 357 & 628 Squadrons, Catalina's.

Much has been written about the air operations involved in connection with the dropping or landing of agents in occupied Europe during World War 2. Little has been written about similar operations in the Far East, where the gathering of intelligence by agents was just as important. If anything, the air operations required to deliver these agents was probably more difficult than in Europe because of the vast distances that had to be covered (from India and Ceylon) and also because of the nature of the terrain into which the agents had to be delivered and the lack of up-to-date maps and charts for some areas.

In this description of some of the operations I was involved in I have drawn upon accounts written by K. A. Merrick and by agent Captain Tan Sri Ibrahim Ismail. The latter was later to become General and Chief of Staff of Malaysian Armed Forces.

In April 1943 Inter Services Liaison Department (ISLD) had sought for means to land agents on the Burmese coast. Submarine travel would take at least a week and the risk was such that aircraft were considered much more suited to the task. No 240 Squadron, whose Catalina's were based at Redhills Lake in Madras, were asked to carry out some of the operations. Two aircraft were stripped of all non-essential equipment in order to increase their endurance and the operation was carried out on the night of 22/23 April. Unfortunately that attempt failed but a second attempt on 25/26 April by the same two aircraft succeeded. One aircraft made a diversionary bombing attack while the second aircraft landed the party. Later operations were to employ similar tactics and in January 1944 two of the squadron's aircraft flew to an island off the South Burma coast. As the Catalina landed both its side blisters were broken and the centre compartment shipped about two feet of sea water, which took three hours to bail out on the return flight. However, the agents had been landed safely and a month later the squadron successfully recovered them and brought them back to India.

In February 1944 No. 357 (Special Duties) Squadron was formed with six Liberators and three Hudson's operating from Digri and six Catalina's (plus three reserves) operating from Redhills Lake in Madras. This separation of flights by 900 miles proved impractical so B Flight became No. 628 (SD) Squadron in March 1944. Five experienced Catalina crews were selected and the C.O., Sqn Ldr. Frank Godber (Six feet six inches tall and aged twenty four) briefed us on the nature of our work which, unlike previous operations, would involve night landings on lakes, rivers, or the open sea without any form of aid. People were allowed to withdraw and some did so, for all crews were made up of volunteers. While the pilots concentrated on practising landing in all weather conditions at night without any flarepath, the crews were sent off for jungle training exercises, with some of the agents. Our flying kit was adapted to include special survival equipment in case we had to land in the jungle and this even included a Kukri (the long wide-bladed knives made famous by the Ghurkas). We also learned the delicate arts of assembling collapsible kayaks (used by the agents to paddle ashore) and of unloading stores from the side blisters of a Catalina into rubber dinghies in a running sea and in total darkness. The aircraft were stripped of all search radar and IFF equipment, so navigators were forced back onto dead-reckoning and astro-navigation techniques. (Their subsequent proficiency earned them top place for accuracy in the No. 255 Group list.)

For very long range trips aircraft were stripped of their armament and extra fuel tanks installed. With stores for the agents and this extra fuel, the take-off run on the water was sometimes prolonged to over two minutes. Take-off was usually around 2300 hours and the aircraft would fly East across the Indian Ocean to about 92 degrees East, then reduce height to 50ft to sneak under the radar screen from the Andaman or Nicobar Islands. If the dropping zone was in the Gulf of Siam, height would be reduced even more as the coast of Malaya was approached.

On 24th October 1944 two Catalina's left Redhills Lake for China Bay in Ceylon to participate in an operation code-named "Oatmeal". The aim was to drop four agents into Malaya, about 1500 miles to the South east. After two days of training with the agents we got airborne at 0630 hours on October 28th , taking off from the open sea outside Trincomalee Harbour. The anti-submarine boom at the harbour entrance was lowered to enable us to do this as our take-off run would have been too long for us to take off within the harbour. Each aircraft carried two agents. All armament, apart from a single .303 machine gun in the nose turret, had been removed. So had the crew's parachutes, as the whole operation was to be flown at heights below 150 ft. so parachutes would be of little use.

We crossed the Malayan coast at about 2000 hours, in bright moonlight, which fortunately enabled the crews to see Japanese aircraft engaged in night-flying practice at a nearby airfield. My skipper, Flight Lieutenant P. A. H. McKeand, who was leading the operation, made a quick decision to temporarily join their circuit in order to avoid detection and W. O .Brooks, in the second aircraft, did likewise. Fortunately this daring ruse was successful and we were able to continue on our way. On reaching Kota Bharu, neither aircraft was able to land because of high seas, so we flew on to the Perhentian Islands where we landed safely. However, an unidentified boat suddenly appeared close by and then sheered off. Unsure now about the security of the operation, we took off and flew back to base with the agents. Both crews re-flew the operation on 31st October and this time landed three of the agents successfully. (The fourth agent was too sick to go ashore.) The return flight brought both crews to the brink of exhaustion for we landed some 31 hours after departure which, I believe, was at that time the longest recorded operational flight in the RAF. Our skipper, Flt Lt McKeand, was awarded a bar to his DFC for this operation.

There was great disappointment a few days later when we received news that the three agents had been captured. What we did not know was that the agents had convinced the Japanese of their pro-Japanese feelings and so begun a long and successful double deception game. Bogus Information was fed to the Japanese throughout the rest of the war. One of those agents, at that time a Captain in the Malayan army, aged 22, later rose to command the post-war Malaysian armed forces.

About this time another of the squadron aircraft was called upon to retrieve some agents who reported that their presence had been discovered and that a party had been landed from a Japanese submarine to search for them. When they reported that the submarine had departed from the bay where they were, an aircraft was dispatched although the crew involved had then flown some seventy hours on three trips in four days. On arrival above the pick-up bay a flashlight signal (from the agents) indicated that it was all clear to land but, while on the downwind leg, the bow turret gunner reported that the submarine was in the middle of the bay. The pilot brought the aircraft in low over the submarine and then taxied fast on the step down-moon in a whirl of spray. Engines had to be cut and an anchor thrown out to enable the agents in their dinghies to come alongside. It seemed that they were unaware of the submarine's presence but the crew shouted to enlighten them and never have rubber dinghies moved so fast! The anchor cable was cut with an axe and the dinghies, with their equipment, were cast adrift. Fortunately the down-moon position of the aircraft prevented its exact position from being discovered and the engines re-started without a splutter. A down-wind take-off took the aircraft straight over the submarine again and then a turn, flat over the water and behind a cliff face, saw the aircraft with the agents safely away on its return to base. For twenty minutes the aircraft had been in an extremely vulnerable situation and the captain, Flt Lt Daymond, was awarded the DSO.

At the end of October 1944 No. 628 Squadron was disbanded because of shortages of aircrew, ground-crew, and equipment. I was in one of the crews who returned to 240 Squadron.

Our next 'special duties' operation was at the beginning of December when we flew as the support and diversionary aircraft on an agent-delivery operation code-named "Biff". On this operation we were also required to search for a Catalina that had been lost on a previous operation but unfortunately we saw no sign of it. Later that month and just before Christmas 1944 our crew took part in a slightly different type of special duties operation. Previous operations had involved delivering or retrieving agents to and from Malaya. This was to be one of a series of operations to Siam (later Thailand).

I believe that plans for these operations to Siam were made jointly with the Americans, for they had been actively involved in political activities which resulted in a pro-Japanese administration in the country being overthrown and replaced by a (clandestinely) pro-allied government, under the rule of a regent who also headed the resistance movement in Siam. So there were a series of special operations which involved delivery or collection of people who were more politically connected than the usual intelligence agents.

We took part in the third of a series of operations code-named "Balmoral". We completed it successfully although our aircraft was slightly damaged when we landed back at base on Christmas Eve, having been airborne for just over twenty-seven hours. The importance of this operation may be judged by the fact that the Allied Air Commander in Chief, South East Asia, sent an immediate signal of congratulations to the skipper and crew. Shortly afterwards Peter McKeand, our skipper, was awarded a bar to his DFC and was promoted to Squadron Leader. Similarly, when the squadron C.O., Wg Cdr Woods, flew with us as captain on a similar operation just one month later, he too was awarded the DFC and the Commander in Chief sent another message of congratulations to the crew.

Catalina

Towards the end of February 1945 we took part in a series of special operations to Siam. Over ten days we flew four operational sorties aggregating over 114 hours flying, of which more than forty hours were spent over enemy occupied territory. Among the people we collected and returned safely nine days later were the former Foreign Minister of Siam, a government official who later became their new Foreign Minister, and the Chief-of-Staff of the Siamese army. These operations resulted in our skipper, Peter McKeand, being awarded the DSO.

Before my tour with 240 Squadron ended at the end of March 1945 I flew on three more similar "special duties" operations, each of which was successful (at least from the RAF side). During my tour I had flown over a thousand hours on Catalina's, of which three hundred and sixty three hours were on "special duties" operations.

HALIFAX AIRCRAFT NO. W 7849

By F/O Skinner 199111. Navigator B.

Whilst waiting in Algiers for a posting to 69 [N.R.] Squadron in Italy, a volunteer navigator was called for- shall we say, "Special Navigational Duties". Never volunteer was the phrase that came to mind at the time. However, my Baltimore aircraft skipper encouraged me to take on the job, "it would keep my hand in" he said, and on March 21st 1944 I was driven over to Maison Blanche, Transport Command, Auth. 144 M.U. and introduced to F/0 Earl. In brief the Halifax aircraft had been modified by extending the bomb doors to accommodate two Merlin engines in the bomb bay.

March 22nd. with F/0 Earl at the Controls and with a W/O WOP he knew very well, [they had completed a tour of Operations together] we took off. I eventually discovered there were not two but three new Merlin engines in the bomb bay. I had already stumbled over numerous aircraft spares in the fuselage in addition several senior RAF officers seated as best able on, and in, aeroplane spares. I presumed the Officers were being transported by us, to take up posts at our destination.

This was my first experience of navigating a large aircraft and the navigation table etc. was a joy to behold. Our destination was Italy - route via C.Bizerte, C.Passero, C.Colonne, Taranto to Brindisi, where we were to unload. Flying time 5hrs 45mins.

I think - but am not absolutely certain - the reason for this exercise was to prove it more economical to change an engine than service an old one in the war theatre for which we were headed. Hence this experimental delivery of new Merlin engines.

Of course, the Italian invasion and big build up was under way, and although I had been trained for G.R and was familiar with Coastal operations I found the dozens of ships we flew around on our way to Italy, an amazing sight to say the least.

March 24th, Having delivered the cargo and spent a couple of nights in Brindis, we took off for Pomigliano Naples, {flying time 1 hr.35mins} where I think we picked up some cargo for the return flight.

March 25th. Night of 24th in Pomigliano, picked up more cargo. Took off for Base via C.Bizerte, flying time 4hrs 4O min.

I was asked to continue this work but as I was already "crewed" felt obliged to refuse the offer and so it was I rejoined my own Crew

Upon reflection the Pregnant Halifax, as she was referred to by the ground crew, did take a long run and time to become airborne when leaving base on its outward journey. I often wondered if this particular work continued and, if so, for how long and when and where it finished.

NOT QUITE CRICKET!

By Rex Hurley of Bournemouth & Peter Burgess of Christchurch

Rex Hurley

In June 1943 I was on my first RAF leave from a Preliminary Air Crew Training Course in Edinburgh. Arriving at my home in Bournemouth and being a very keen cricketer, I contacted Bowmakers, Lloyds Bank and Kennedys (all of whom I'd played for in civvy street) and on Saturday, 5 June turned out for Lloyds for an afternoon match at Kings Park.

I was just running up to bowl when four or five Me 109s swept in and banked very low over us. I remember waving to them and getting a wave back from one of the EAs and, looking round the field, practically everyone had flattened or run for cover .to the nearby trees. I recall thinking, little do they know about fighters, as long as they don't point their noses at us we can't be hit by their machine guns or cannons (and also wondered if I bowled and hit the stumps, whether I could claim the wicket?).

Suddenly it dawned on me that some Me109s were fighter - bombers and could carry a 250 lb bomb, so I hadn't been as sensible as my team mates after all. (What a target we would have made in our 'whites' against a green background!)

Fifty odd years later, I was sitting with friends round a table at one of our fortnightly Air Crew Association meetings at the Flying Club, Hurn Airport, when a friend, Peter Burgess, suddenly announced that he'd been playing cricket one Saturday in Kings Park, He was just running up to bowl when an Me 109 interrupted play and the pilot waved to them. (There were three cricket matches being played in the park; Peter was at the Ashley Road end whilst we were playing at the Football Club end.) We checked our diaries which confirmed the date and location. What an incredible coincidence!

Peter Burges

At 1300 hrs on Sunday, 23 May, 1943, I was coming out of the school in Lowther Road, which was the 130 Sqdn ATC Headquarters, when an FW 190, flying at rooftop height, came up the road from Holdenhurst Road and opened fire with its cannon. Needless to say, I hit the deck pretty quickly.

Then nearly a fortnight later, on the afternoon of Saturday, 5 June, I was playing cricket against the Pay Corps at Kings Park. As I ran up to bowl, an Me 109, flying at 30 ft, came from the direction of Ashley Road gates, between our cricket pitch and the pavilion. The pilot raised his left hand in salute, or perhaps he was hoping to make a catch at fine slip, but he was probably thinking, don't they know there's a bloody war on.

I found out a couple of years ago that Rex Hurley was on the next pitch, facing the opposite direction to me and saw a different view of the raid by five more Me109s.

The following month, I was called up for aircrew training and so ended an exciting month for an 18 year-old.

First published in May 1999 in the Wartime News and reproduced here by kind permission of the editor.

EPITAPHS

This airforce `Erk` by the name of John Sharp
Wanted wings, he got `em and now plays a harp

Here lies the body of pilot Von Braddit
A Spitfire got him so that's how he had it

In memoriam of Flying Officer Bell
Who dived too low and landed in hell

In memory of Bomber Brown
Who fell from his plane and is on his way down

In memory of Wireless Op. Clash
Who pressed a wrong button and went up in a flash

From this plane fell A/G Crownlet
He left us last night and hasn't got down yet

Here lies the body of bomb maker Brown
Who was blown up in the air and never came down

RAF POST WAR

John Moss

The war was over. I enjoyed my flying and decided to remain in the RAF so I signed on as a regular SNCO Pilot. A total of twelve years would pass flying military aircraft before I made the decision to change my career and venture into the outside world of Civvy Street.

My request to fly Jet Fighters was granted. I joined 266 Sqdn based at Tangmere. My conversion from Hurricanes to the Meteor Mk.3 would take place on the Squadron. It was quite straight forward, a dual flight in an Oxford aircraft to give me some multi-engined experience, the Flight Commander as Captain, this was followed by a verbal check on Flight Procedures & Aircraft handling notes. No problems and I was soon airborne in my first Jet.

A few months later the R.A.F's first so called "High Speed Jet" was coming into service. The new Meteor Mk.4. with clipped wings, high power, high speed (600mph plus), high altitude, high Speed Navigation. Well it was in those days. I was very lucky, I was selected to join the very first conversion course. Gloucesters Chief Test Pilot, Bill Waterton, turned up at beginning of course to give a verbal introduction on the merits of this new high speed jet. Its capabilities and also High speed problems etc. All very impressive at the time (I am going back over fifty years). Having completed the course, I returned to Tangmere feeling very pleased having flown the R.A.F's fast new aircraft. It really was a delight to fly the Meteor Mk.4.

Some time later I was in one of three Mk.4's in formation. Our task was to carry out attacks on an airborne Sunderland flying boat using the aircraft's camera gun. When it was my turn I commenced my 'Curve of pursuit' from slightly above and towards the Port side of flying boat. My approach speed was fast, very fast, too bloody fast and I was too close to the target. I increased the back pressure on the control column. The G forces were high and I kept my tummy muscles taut. My body pressed firmly in my seat and back rest and my vision became blurred. The 'thud' I heard was very loud and clear. I knew something serious had happened so I relaxed pressure on the stick. Pressure reduced on body and full vision returned. From the instrument panel was one very red warning light indicating that my Port undercarriage was unlocked. I immediately reduced power, extended Air Brakes to reduce speed to 175 knots, the maximum for undercarriage in the down position. I obviously had a problem so I pressed the radio button to advise base of my situation. No contact could be made as my radio was dead and I now had two problems, the undercarriage and the radio.

I headed back to Tangmere gradually losing altitude, keeping the airspeed at 175 knots . My thoughts centred on my Port undercarriage. In view of high G imposed on aircraft, was my undercarriage down and locked or was it the micro switch which operated the red light that was faulty?. Should I chance a wheels down landing or wheels up?. I joined the circuit, it was all mine as unknown to me all aircraft had been recalled and landed. I checked the visual signals area which showed a right hand circuit in use and the short runway for landing. I made three low passes over the Control Tower at 200/250ft tipping both wings separately still keeping my airspeed at 175 knots, knowing my situation was being assessed from the ground and action taken accordingly. At the same time I was also reducing my fuel content which was very important in this situation. I had already decided my course of action, I would make a low power approach on the short runway, with my undercarriage selected down and 30 degree flap but with my airspeed a little higher than normal. Should the undercarriage hold on touchdown, I would select full flap and throttle back. If there was any tendency to sink then I had sufficient speed and power to overshoot and go round for a wheels up landing.

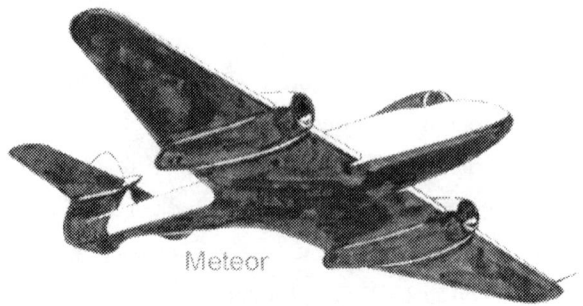

It seemed right at the time after all we did many touch downs and overshoots during our early training days. On touchdown the wheels were firmly on runway so I quickly throttled back and selected full flap. As the speed reduced the port wing started to drop, and drop, and drop. Too late to overshoot I applied full starboard rudder and some brake, which was effective in braking the starboard wheel. With careful use of the brakes I had no difficulty in keeping the aircraft on the runway, despite the wing tip being only inches off the runway surface. The aircraft came to a halt a few yards short of the end of runway. Immediate inspection showed Port Undercarriage Hydraulic Jack (which raised and lowered the undercarriage) had broken. This allowed the leg to move sideways, both left and right. I did not consider this could happen when I was airborne, who would have?. As the speed reduced after touchdown the undercarriage leg had moved to the left under the engine nacelle, so keeping the port wing tip just off the surface of the runway. All Meteor Mk.4's were immediately grounded.

Later investigation showed the undercarriage locking device was faulty under high G loading. All aircraft were modified and if memory correct the flying ban was lifted 3 to 4 weeks later. After making my report there were no further comments from my seniors. For me the matter was closed. I remained on Squadron for a total of thirteen months to be followed by a course at the Central Flying School to become a Q.F.I.. a tour of four years instructing lay ahead. Two years up to the Wings standard and two years on Jet Conversion including the odd incident of course, that's a part of Military Flying, Happy days

TENACITY PAYS OFF

Charlie Joy

My aircrew experience was a very placid affair, but my RAF service began in 1928 as I will explain. I attended the RAF Air Display at Hendon in 1927, 1928 and 1929. The last visit in RAF uniform, which was "cheese-cutter" cap, high neck tunic and pantaloons and puttees. We also carried a swagger cane. This proved to be my last outing for over a year, as will be explained later.

I left school at the end of 1927 and commenced work in a private garden, hard work, long hours and peanut wages. But I was determined to become a technical apprentice (a Brat) at RAF Halton. Unfortunately my school education was not advanced enough to pass the entrance exam. So I went to a Technical School teacher, for two hours one evening a week, for which I paid half a crown (12 new pence today). He set me homework, but I used to go to sleep over my books in the evening, after a hard days work. So I used to rise at 5a.m. and do my studying before going to work at 7 o'clock, I was dead keen!.

In May, I asked my tutor if I could sit the exam and I still remember his words, "Boy, you haven't got a snowball in Hells chance". But when he heard that I could have three attempts, he told me to take it, to see how much I still had to learn. Unfortunately I passed (about 250 from 600) and as a result was at a disadvantage when joining the others. This was in August 1928, when I was enrolled A/A 562759 and based with C Squadron, 2 Wing, No 1 School of Technical Training RAF Halton. I know that Paddy Mahon and Tug Wilson followed me there.

Discipline was tough. I trained as an Aero Engine Fitter until July 1929, when I was admitted to Princess Mary's Hospital with fluid on a stiff knee. I was kept in bed for 10 months, during which my other knee developed trouble. I returned to training in September 1930, when I was put back three entries. But after a medical check-up, I was returned to hospital until December. I then faced a medical board and was discharged as, medically unfit. You can imagine my disappointment. The Chairman of the board was an RAF surgeon, Sqd. Ldr. Hall. I was to meet him again in Ceylon in 1945, when he was Air Commodore Hall.

I volunteered for Air Crew in 1941, and was accepted after tests, including a medical. My medical discharge papers were cancelled and I was called up to A.C.R.C. in February 1942, as u/t Navigator. After I.T.W. at Babbacombe, some of us were posted to Cranwell for wireless operator training which we did not want. We were tested at the end of the course when the pass mark was 60%. None of our course made it, so the papers were called in by the Chief Examiner and we were all re-assessed at 60.5%. During this time we were tested in the decompression chamber and during it I had aches in my knee, which I reported, as a result I was banned from high flying. We passed out as Navigator/Bomb Aimer/Wireless Operators in the Isle of Man in May 1943.

Owing to congestion in the training chain, I was posted to 15(P) A.F.U. at Greenham Common where I flew with many newly trained pilots from Canada. That autumn I was posted to Ceylon via Bombay on a troop ship, and arrived just before Christmas 1943. I was then sent up country to Vavunya to join 22 Sqdn flying Beauforts in Coastal Command. We were entirely defensive until converting to Beaufighters and then we converted to a strike role. We trained at a rocket range, but my pilot and I were taken off the squadron, having completed twelve months. This was just before they were posted to the Arakan. Their losses were very heavy, so I was very lucky to have had that transfer.

I then joined S.E.A.C. Communications squadron at Colombo, flying in Beechcraft Expeditors. My first and only trip with them was to take Air Marshal Jubert to Calcutta, Tamu and Delhi on a P.R. tour lasting ten days. On my return I joined 222 Group Communications Flight and stayed with them until I came home in March 1946. We made many taxi runs all over India with V.I.P's. I met up with my training companions at Alipore with 484 Sqd P.R.U., and also met Air Commodore Hall again. But our aircraft was reserved for AVM Breakey, the A.O.C. Ceylon. When the Japs packed up he became A.O.C. Malaya and flew to Singapore in a Sunderland. Our range was limited so we had a leisurely trip visiting Madras, Calcutta, Rangoon, Bangkok, and Penang arriving at Singapore after 6 days. Later we were based at Kuala Lumpur and nearly all our flights were to airfields in Malaya. I did go to Sumatra and Batavia (Jakarta) where we took Group Captain Edwards VC to take over as A.O.C. Indonesia.

I returned to England in another troopship in March 46, and was demobbed near Preston in time for Easter. I had flown with 171 pilots by that time. I was a Founder Member of the Bournemouth Branch ACA at Boscombe in 1979, I believe this was the first branch and H.Q. at Wool were not very happy about it. I seldom attend meetings now for my deafness makes conversation difficult in a crowded room, but I still attend Remembrance parade at Bournemouth War Memorial.

P.S. I was invited to Fairford in 1998 to represent the 1928 entry to the RAF's 80th Birthday.

AIRCREW - Times Past

Life was a fleeting moment when
We lived from day today
A moment dawned, the sun broke through,
We savoured every ray,
For well we knew that, with the dusk
There was a price to pay.
When we were young.

The danger that we faced became
A common bond to share
The friendships forged upon such fire
Were rich beyond compare
So many of them all too short
Their loss so hard to bear
When we were young.

We lived our lives up to hilt
We laughed and loved and prayed
We learned to crack the flippant joke
If we should feel afraid,
These things were all accepted
As by us the rules were made,
When we where young.

So many years have passed since then,
The flames of war have died,
The individual paths we chose
Are scattered far and wide.
But we remember proudly those
Whose lives to ours were tied
When we were young.

THE NIGHT OF AUGUST 30-31 1943

By George Flanagan

The attack came from the stern and below. The gunners engaged the stern attacker but the one underneath, with up-firing guns, got us. They were both ME's and we were well alight on the port side. The command was loud and clear from Johnnie, our skipper. "Prepare to abandon aircraft". I clipped on my 'chute and then, "Abandon aircraft, I can't hold her", his last command to us. Les, our Mid-upper, was talking on the intercom then sudden silence. Jock, our rear-gunner, couldn't rotate his turret as the port inner engine was well alight and this controlled the hydraulics. Bob, our Flight Engineer, started back along the aircraft to help Jock. Sid, the Navigator, calmly folded his seat, Jack the Wop. stood up and I moved back near the escape position; Jonnie wrestled all the time with the now useless controls. Suddenly the aircraft lurched over and there was a flash. I was thrown against the inside of the aircraft and I remember no more.

I came to flying through the air, cold on my face, the 'chute clipped to my chest. I pulled the D-ring and the chute opened. It broke my fall although I hit the ground very hard, falling through some trees. My flying boots had come off but I never found out where. I lay there winded but alive, and wondered if I was the only one. I could hear the aircraft above returning to their bases. The impossible had happened. Most aircrew adopted the attitude it might happen to somebody else, but not us. But it had happened to us!

After a while I tried to pull the 'chute down from the tree, but it was fixed so I gave up and reached for my cigarette case in my top left battle-dress pocket, only to find it was bent in half. I must have struck something hard. I found the remnants of a cigarette, scooped out a couple of handfuls of earth and bent down and lit it. I thought I must move away from where I had landed but found that I couldn't walk, so I crawled. I came to a barbed wire fence in the woods, clambered over it as well as I could and landed on the other side. As I hit the deck a shot rang out. I got up and ran about half a dozen steps in fear, then collapsed.

Firstly, two German shepherd dogs ran up snarling and showing their teeth. Then a German-style home guard was next. He struck me in the back with his rifle and indicated that he wanted me to empty my pockets. I was about to do this when up came a soldier who took over. He assisted me in walking to a woodland road nearby where a Volkswagen was parked. He pushed me in and then we drove off. After a while we stopped near a cultivated field where there were people and other soldiers. I could see the wreckage of an aircraft everywhere, which obviously was ours, and as I got closer I could make out three bodies.

Jack the Wop was killed on impact, his 'chute, still packed, clipped to his chest. Les, the Mid-upper, had been hit in the head by a bullet and Jock, our rear-gunner, was lying halfway out of the remains of his turret. No sign of John the skipper, Sid the Nav or Bob the Flight Engineer.

I was then driven to the village at Rheydt, still with no boots. As I sat in the jail, I thought I must be the only one to survive. Suddenly there was a lot of noise, opening and shutting of doors and so on, and then Bob the Flight Engineer was pushed into the cell. I told him about the others although, I think, we were both still too dazed to take it all in. Later on that day another airman was brought in; he said he was a Navigator on Lancs. He asked too many questions so we kept quiet and he was then taken out of the cell.

After a couple of days, washing our faces and hands in a little brook that ran by the side of the jail, and trying to stomach their potato and chive stew with dark brown soggy bread, a couple of Luftwaffe guards called to take us by train to Dulag Luft, in Frankfurt, the interrogation centre. We travelled in with the passengers. When we arrived at Frankfurt station, we met up with airmen shot down on the Berlin raid that took place the night after our Monchengladbach raid. As we were in the station a menacing crowd started to move towards us. The Luftwaffe guards got five of us in to the waiting room, one chap had lost a foot, one had two broken arms and such a swollen face he couldn't see, and three of us couldn't walk. They then stood in front of the others and fired pistols over their heads; this dispersed them. There we waited nervously for transport to Dulag Luft, the interrogation centre.

Dulag Luft was a showpiece, good food, cigarettes tea coffee and quite good sleeping accommodation, in fact a nice chatty atmosphere while the Germans listened. Certainly for Bob and I it was a bonus because, after we'd been there a day, Sid our Navigator was brought in. So we then knew three of us were safe. He knew no more than us how he got out of the aircraft.

Then came my turn for interrogation by a young German Luftwaffe officer who spoke perfect English. We had always been told to give name, rank and number plus denomination, nothing else. He said what was your civilian occupation and I replied that I was a plumber's mate and refused to say more. He got very agitated, snatched back the cigarette he gave me and said something like, "You English airmen are all the same, students, coalmen, dustmen and labourers" and then ushered me out of the room. Interrogation finished. Before all this however, he seemed to have great pride in the fact that he could tell me all about our 77 Squadron and a lot of its members, including our crew. The Germans must have had a marvellous intelligence system.

The next day we left in closed railway cattle trucks, for 6 horses or 50 men, en-route for Stalag IVB, Muhlberg-on-Elbe. The trip took three days and nights and was the biggest nightmare of all. The officers went to Stalag Luft III, including our Sid who was a Flying Officer.

Stalag IVB Muhlberg was very close to the River Elbe, about 60 miles SSW of Berlin. It was situated in what many years ago had been the bed of a lake. It was originally a Russian POW camp but an outbreak of typhus had closed it. We were the first POW's to re-occupy it. Later on we were to see many

Fortress raids to Berlin, one Fortress crew-member baled out from an aircraft in trouble and landed in the middle of our camp. We also witnessed night raids on Berlin, Leipzig and Dresden etc including the firestorm raid on Dresden. It became quite obvious that whilst in prison camp you had to find something to do. I was taught the guitar (later described) and I was also taught to play bridge by Cyril Bicknell. He and I won many cigarettes (our currency). Eventually 5 of us used to dish out the German rations for the other 235 POW's in our hut. On such meagre rations, I consider this was quite an honour.

Our Camp Stalag IVB was finally liberated by the Russians in April 1945. Two officers of the Red Army arrived, smoking American cigarettes and said that this part of Germany was in Russian hands. We broke out of camp and in small gangs went searching for food. We found a sunken barge on the side of the river Elbe. It was full of cases of evaporated milk in small tins. We took some cases of milk to the Polish women.

The Russians, after a few days made us pick up our belongings, assemble, then marched us down to Reisa on the river Elbe. As we went along their troops came through going down to Czechoslovakia to fight the German pockets of resistance there. It was absolute chaos. We were eventually installed in a disused German army barracks in Reisa, the Russians then posted an armed guard around the barracks and refused to let us out so Bicknell, Dickson, Ganett, Wilkins and myself escaped.

After many various happenings, some with trigger happy Russian support troops, not the Red Army, demanding food from the German villages and Schloss's, tip toeing your way through thousands of displaced refugees sandwiched between the advancing American and Russian armies we reached the American front line. The outfit was the 103rd division "The Timber wolves". They fed us on C and K rations. We were then transported to Halle and then flown back to Brussels with a number of other airmen by the American Air Force, in Dakotas.

In Brussels we met up with the Dalmote family, a unit of the Belgian underground who had helped Wilkins to hide from the Germans after he was shot down and injured. So we went A.W.O.L. and stayed with them for a couple of days. The father, Papa Dalmote showed us an armoury of guns and grenades etc. he had reserved for the collaborators who had worked with the Germans.

Eventually the RAF flew us back to England in Lancaster's. They were marvellous to us and couldn't do enough for us. Having food and drink served to you by lovely W.A.A.Fs and high ranking officers, it was a real reception. We then entrained to Stamford for re-kitting out and were then given back pay and eight weeks leave. Eventually I was de-mobbed from Hednesford RAF station.

At home they arranged a Welcome Home Party for me. We were also invited to a garden party at Buckingham Palace.

A WEEK TO REMEMBER

By George Flanagan

From the pencil notes and diary of his friend the late W/O Bill Plunket also of 77 Sqdn. whilst at Stalag IVB

STALAG IVb Situated on the River ELBE.
Dresden situated 26 miles SE of camp

Leipzig	32	W of camp
Berlin	68	N of camp.
Torgau	10	NW of camp. Where Russians and American forces linked

DIARY OF EVENTS.

17th April 1945. Tuesday These past few days have brought excitement and anxiety to quite a few of the POW's in IVb. Since the handing over of the camp's internal administration by the Lt. Col. to Lt. Jessop (British) on Friday 13th following a scare of Allies in the Torgau area, a feeling of expectancy and great tension has been felt. Throughout each day Allied aircraft have been continually witnessed, some in action. some just stooging. In all, the lads appear to be having a helluva fine time and many an envious eye may have been gazing upwards.

Previous to the day's attack the target has always been outside the precincts of the camp, ie, barges on the Elbe, rolling stock along the line and the not too distant aerodrome. Thunderbolts, Mustangs and Lightnings have been the type used. Yesterday's attack was made on a goods train that was travelling North-South, half a mile distance from the camp. A wood fatigue party, approx. 100 men, when nearing the railway crossing became the unwelcome spectators of a first class shoot-up by the Yanks on the train that was crawling along the line some 2-300 yards ahead. The first kite dropped a bomb ahead of the loco, bringing it to a halt. The following attack saw the loco. destroyed by point 5 calibre machine gun fire. Then systematic strafing of the trucks commenced. The flak barrage put up didn't worry our boys at all, complete destruction was the common verdict of eye witnesses. Attack - took place at about 1.35pm, but it wasn't until 2315 hrs that the railway line was in action again,

Today a very unfortunate shoot up took place at around 1115 hrs, Another wood fatigue party was returning with their loads of wood when two Mustangs attacked them, just near the camp main gate. They attacked from about 3000 ft suddenly diving and firing a burst at the leaders, being at the top of the camp (W) towards the main camp area - causing panic among the 20,000 inhabitants. Three of the wood fatigue party were killed and one German guard. Bullets penetrated several barracks in camp inflicting some wounds. One chap who was shaving in the alleyway beside his bed was chipped in the back of the neck with a .5 calibre coming at an angle through the roof. During the afternoon much aircraft activity was observed, the lads have been aircraft wary these past few hours and the direction of the kites and their subsequent movement being closely followed, 1500-1600 hours. Formation of Lightnings and Thunderbolts circled the area several times, finally heading NW at 6-7000 ft, Later around 1800 hrs again circled and dived and attacked in the direction of the Elbe, presumably barges. Night activity consisted of an alarm from 2300 hrs till 0300 hrs,

18th April. Wednesday. Formation of 12 Me.109`s and FW 190's flew over camp at 200 ft. heading south - a rare sight these days - as Jerry aircraft have become almost non existent these days, 0820 hrs large formation of

Thunderbolts. Lightnings and Mustangs appeared in the vicinity of the camp, 3-4000 ft which was the height of cloudbase, and continually patrolled throughout the day. 1600 hrs more fighters strafing anything on or near the river Elbe. Camp Security has commenced by the display of a 40 ft x 10 ft POW sign on what we call the rugby pitch. Roofs to be painted also. 1800 hrs. Heavy raid by formation of bombers up to 8 miles N of camp believed to be Falkenburg. Fighters appeared to S of camp approx. 10-15 miles away. Both raids coinciding. Weather dismal with grey sky. 1820 hrs. Fighters strafed some 5 miles away to SW of camp probably barges on the Elbe. Yank Thunderbolt pilot in barracks shot down yesterday in Leipzig area - stated all pilots and crews are informed of the camp area and warned to stay clear. Yesterdays performance probably due to the pilot mistaking wood fatigue party for camouflaged Jerry's. 1900 hrs Thunderbolts over camp area. Sky clearing visibility good. Strafing area previously bombed and area of the Elbe. Russian offensive had large gains made to within 20 miles of Berlin. Night alarm 2200 hrs - 0300 hrs.

19th April Thursday. Radio reports Russians within 15 Kms, of Dresden - brings things nearer here than ever – feelings running high. Much fighter activity observed after 0830 hrs. Strafing target some few miles N.E of camp. 10-30 hrs large formation of heavies seen flying over camp (Fortresses) with fighter escort observed. Some bombed Falkenburg and some somewhere else. Some 20-30 minutes after a terrific explosion followed by fire took place at target. Fighter activity continued throughout the morning, little air activity during afternoon. Note Jerry has put an anti-tank gun midway along W. boundary of camp. Rumours of fall of Leipzig and Welmar 20Km, SW. Eight Thunderbolts provided entertainment this evening at 1830 hrs. Four trucks had been in the siding in the woods near the camp for the last 5 days and an engine had just been tacked on to them to pull them off when the fighters spotted it. They attacked the train from N to S. along the line 200yds from camp. When the fun had attracted all the POW`s to the wire - the kites put on a show by continuing the shoot up from W. to E. along the camp boundary at various heights, 1000ft down to 200ft and about 300 yds, N. of the camp explosions indicated that it was an ammo. train, These continued to about 1930 hrs with odd ex-plosions all night. Lights in camp are put on all night these days,

20th April Friday. Fall of Leipzig reported. MPs to visit Welmar, Advances of Russian and Allies towards Dresden and Berlin. Thunderbolts and other fighters noticed at 0830 hrs about 3000ft above camp, very active. Large explosions seen and heard about 10 miles S. of camp in the direction of Reisa, During the afternoon more fighters observed. 1500 hrs. Large column of smoke some 8 miles NW. 1600 hrs. Very many large explosions some six to eight miles to south. Maybe demolition by Jerry, but fighters were in vicinity. 1800 hrs. Continuous heavy rumbling from direction of Torgaut, opinion that it is artillery about 8 - 10 miles NW. Heavy pall of smoke over area. 2000 hrs. Skyline to south of camp being continually lit up in direction coinciding with that of 1600 hrs explosions. Explosions which were estimated at Reisa unlike the latter, no reports were heard. (Some say demolition, some say artillery). 2105 hrs. Parachute flares seen over area. Glow from big fires in that area. Much excitement in barrack room with rum-ours that Jerry had left camp. (Found out to be wrong). 2300 hrs. Reports that meeting had taken place with Lt. Col, Koenig (German Commandant) and all nationals except Russian. The reason being that in view of the present rapid rate of advance of the Russian forces towards the area, do we wish to be evacuated across the Elbe? emphatic NO by British and AmerIcans followed by other Nationals except Poles, who wouldn't listen. Col. Koenig then said he wasn't sure whether all or only some of his guards would be evacuated. 2330 hrs. Statement that all sentries and guards were remaining and apart from the immediate evacuation of the Poles, (700 men), camp routine to be as usual. Allies on outskirts of Dresden, Russians 25Kms E. of Dresden.

21st April Saturday. 0630 hrs. Jerry jet flew low over camp (very rare these days). 0700 hrs roll-call as usual. Very cloudy morning, aircraft heard but low ceiling and weather murky. Noted absence of prominent Jerry guards and rest have strained appearances and are packed ready to move, 1130 hrs to-day's bread ration not to be issued until further supplies arrive from Muhlberg, transport problem is the reason. Only one 3 tonne lorry in use as the others are gas operated and only being used from dusk to dawn owing to raids. It`s sufficient to supply 20,000 men. 1230 hrs. Red Cross reports a clearout from POW parcel magazine, approximately 14 cigs, and 2 articles per 5 men for issue on Monday - amid cheers, issuing is to be made sometime this afternoon.

1730 hrs Gen. Eisenhower's message "Link up with the Russians expected In a few days, "STAY PUT" Afternoon dreary, occasional showers. German Commandant reports Russian advance to train line Berlin to Dresden- at Juterbog, Column of smoke and continuous rumbling from the direction of Torgau. Eisenhower's message to internees, foreign workers and POW`s. "Only a few days, stay put" raised morale in IVb, Many have started looking through the wire, waiting. Since the 19th no rail traffic on the main line near camp confirms cutting of line by the Russians. Column of smoke from Zeithain area 6 - 8 miles SE of camp. Tension somewhat relieved by arrival of bread ration in camp, 25O grammes per man, Electricity supply ceased at 2200 hrs and off goes water supply. So we have to rely on wells and hand pumps now. Curfew as before,

22nd April, Sunday. Jerry kite flew low over camp this morning. Fairly cold and trying to snow. Our own aircraft conspicuous by their absence, Columns of refugees moving along both roads towards Muhlberg, Jerry column moving N. 88mm guns, tanks and armoured cars, Influx of some thousands of POW`s into camp, Serbs and French last night and early morning. About 1500 POWs in old Danish compound. We have been overcrowded since before Christmas. So things are getting a bit pushed now. 3000 more Russians in, put under canvas on our so- called football pitch. And about 1600 British have also come in, Persistent rumours of Russians being within 20Kmm of camp, 1330 hrs. Another German armoured column moving through, the same strength as before. 1500 hrs. Hungarian guards re-enforced Jerries around perimeter, nervous tension increasing hourly, atmosphere electric, Bridgehead 15Kms. NW across Elbe. Another message from General

Eisenhower. "Remain put, don't take up arms - don't lose hope". All POW's under military law. Internal camp administration comes into action. Special police force formed to maintain guard, As soon as Jerry evacuates, place will be taken by guards, Russians have been wired off separately, Russian Officers in camp try and maintain order among their own prisoners. Precautions have been taken to try and maintain order as there are quite a number of other Nationals, ie Dutch, French, Yugoslavs, Serbs, Belgians, Italians, Yanks. Indians, Cypriots etc.

1600 hrs German tanks, armoured cars and infantry observed passing camp. 500 grams of potatoes, (three times the normal daily amount) to be issued in lieu of bread, as soon as they are cooked. Weather dismal, local showers, cold. Electricity and water still off. Throughout the afternoon explosions appertaining to the demolition of munitions has taken place locally. 2200 hrs. Persistent rumours to the effect that Germans will be evacuating camp area tonight. 2210 hrs. Arrival of some 2-3000 further Russian POW`s. General opinion is that Allied forces will have taken over in the morning.

Russian force rumoured to be within 10 kms. of camp, Majority of prisoners too excited to sleep but strict curfew imposed.

23rd April Monday. German guards and sentries observed evacuating, minor explosions also artillery fire causes barracks to rock and shake. 0200 hrs. Local machine gun and mortar fire, scattered few light artillery rounds - much speculation if we are in the battle area. 0400 hrs. Start security watch in huts. Local activity has died down, or so it appears. Russian troops reported to be in the area. 0530 hrs Previous report confirmed as Russian horse drawn vehicles observed moving along main road running past camp, 0630 hrs. Reveille. 0635 hrs fall in. 0700 hrs. Some semblance of parade but disbanded immediately as the lads rushed to welcome entry of Russian horsemen on local farm horses. Russian POW`s leave, smashed down the wire. All British and Americans told not to leave camp. Raid on potato dump in camp. Lads pouring out of camp all ways. Evidently Jerries from the camp left it too late and have had it, Numerous bodies around in the fields and slain farmstock. Reports seem to indicate no link between Americans and Russians. Fighting breaking out to SW of camp. Artillery fire heard from camp. 1500 hrs. Bags of refugees around with children, trucks, prams etc. Crees and Norman came In with 3 Jerry prisoners.1510 hrs. Russian officers report link-up with Americans expected hourly. Russian, British, American, French, Belgian and Italian flags fly at the main gate.

LIBERATION DAY
MONDAY APRIL 23RD--- ST. GEORGES DAY.

What a day. Serbs have left the camp. A strange experience and we will never have to experience another night like it. Had a walk outside the camp today, sights are pretty horrible. Still no light or water.

24th April Tuesday. Most of the boys out today getting food. Russian troops will give you anything you can eat or carry when you get outside. George and some of the boys found a barge beached on the bank of the river Elbe, it was full of cases of tinned milk. They brought a load back to camp.

REPORTED MISSING

By R. B. Spencer-Fleet, Flight Engineer, 620 Squadron, Stirling's

The date was 30th July 1943 and several crews from 620 Squadron had been briefed that day to take part in an attack on Remscheid, an industrial town south of the Ruhr. The squadron was based at Chedburgh, together with No 246, another Stirling squadron, which also contributed to Bomber Command's main effort that night.

The bomb load was all incendiaries and take-off commenced at 22.30 hours. We climbed to operational height, which in our case was about 13,000 feet, and headed out across the channel. Crossing the Belgian coast in the Bruges/Ostend area we encountered heavy flak. The pilot started weaving, as was normal over enemy territory, but flew level for a short period as the navigator wanted to get a Gee fix. We had been on our course across Belgium for about thirty minutes and, apart from a few searchlights, all seemed to be going well. Then suddenly there was a loud explosion, which caused the aircraft to shudder violently, and at the same time the tail-end of the fuselage erupted in flames. The mid-upper gunner called to the skipper over the intercom that we were being attacked by a fighter from the port-side under and immediately he put the aircraft into a steep dive to starboard. I saw that the pilot had the aircraft under control so, from my position at the flight engineer's panel, I grabbed a nearby fire extinguisher and then told him that I was going down to the burning rear fuselage. As I approached the rear turret the ammunition started to explode. The fire was so intense that the extinguisher had no effect on it. It was clear that the rear gunner had died at the instant of the attack. At this time I had no intercom connection and I was suddenly aware that the Bomb Aimer was tugging at my harness and shouting "Bail out". We made our way back to the front of the aircraft, by which time the Pilot had jettisoned the bombs and the other crew members were attaching their parachutes. I went down into the Bomb Aimer's position and released the forward hatch before returning to get my own parachute. The crew started to evacuate immediately, with the Wireless Operator (who had been mortally wounded, although we did not know this at the time) going first, followed by the mid-upper gunner, the Navigator, and the Bomb-Aimer. During this time the Pilot had managed to keep the aircraft straight and level. I spoke to him and he said that he was alright and that I should get out. I did not need a second invitation as by this time the rear fuselage was burning fiercely.

The whole episode, from the time that the aircraft was attacked until it crashed into the ground in flames, took just eight minutes. I know this because since the war I have obtained a copy of the 'Flugbuch' of Werner Uhlmann, who was the Gunner of the Messerschmitt Bf 110 that shot us down. This nightfighter was from the second squadron of the NJG 4, operating from it's base at Florennes in the Ardennes.

The forward hatchway in the Stirling was big, permitting me, after grabbing the 'D' ring of my 'chute, to tumble out head first from the bottom step. My first impression after the initial rush of air and noise, was of absolute silence, plus an awareness that my left foot was very cold because my boot had been wrenched off as I tumbled from the aircraft. It was a starlit night and I could clearly see the river below me, but nothing else – just complete darkness. There was no sensation of falling and I began to think that I might never get down. When I did reach the ground I struck it with a tremendous jolt, back first.. Fortunately there was little or no wind and as my parachute collapsed I was able to release it without difficulty, then conceal it under some nearby bushes. I had no idea where I was but felt fortunate that I had not landed in a built-up area. All I could hear was the sound of a train whistle in the distance.

While it was dark I decided to get as far away as possible from where I had landed, fearing that there would soon be search parties out. So I walked, wearing just one boot but fortunately it was quite easy going and mainly grassland. At daybreak I found myself on high ground looking over open countryside with a lane below me and a small river about a quarter of a mile beyond that. As I made my way down, wondering what to do next, I heard voices coming from the road. Keeping cover behind a hedgerow I saw a man and a woman approaching. When I realised that they were speaking French and not German I made a quick decision to reveal myself and seek their help. I did not have to speak the language to explain who or what I was. When I broke cover and stood in front of them wearing my RAF battledress with brevet and stripes, sporting a tartan scarf (which I used to wear for luck) and still with one flying boot on, they must have realised immediately that I was from the aircraft that had crashed in flames a few hours earlier. The man caught hold of me and quickly pushed me behind the hedgerow. We communicated with difficulty but I soon realised that they were going to work and must be on their way. However, the man indicated that he could help me and that I should stay where I was until he returned. As they departed along the lane I felt thankful that I had made friendly contact so quickly yet felt very anxious about what lay ahead.

I did not have to wait long for the next development. Within an hour the man returned and indicated that I must move as quickly as possible. As best as I could understand him, the young woman had not been able to resist telling her friends about her experience and he was afraid that the Germans would soon learn my whereabouts. Wishing me "Bon chance" he departed without delay.

Monsieur Roger WAUTELET

I made for the river beyond the field skirting the road. Seeing two men working in the field beyond the river I crossed the field almost flat on my stomach and dropped down a bank into a shallow stream. Now hidden by the bank I waded about a quarter of a mile until, seeing a large house on the opposite bank, I crossed the stream and then crawled to where I could see the house more clearly. After watching for a while and seeing no activity, I approached the house through a large vegetable garden and came to an outhouse. Then I heard someone crossing the yard at the back of the house. As I flattened myself into a recess in the thick stone wall a man pushing a wheelbarrow passed within a few feet of me. He gave me a brief nod but gave no other signs of his awareness of my presence. This I took to be a good omen and felt it was safe for me to cross the courtyard and knock on the rear door of the house. It was opened by a homely-looking woman, probably in her early sixties. Her face at first showed surprise and shock, but that changed to an expression of welcome as she put out her arms, pulled me quickly inside, and closed the door. Now inside a well furnished room, a man (probably her husband) showed equal surprise at my appearance. However, with some English they made me welcome and gave me some food, telling me that they would get in touch with someone who would help me. Seeing that I was exhausted they made me rest on a chaise lounge and I fell fast asleep.

Early in the afternoon I was awakened by a well dressed man who spoke good English and questioned me very closely. Once he was satisfied about my identity he apologised and explained that , because the Germans sometimes planted agents posing as RAF aircrew in order to penetrate the Resistance and discover escape routes, they had to take great care. He then said he could arrange for me to cross the border into Belgium and that in order to do so I would have to change into civilian clothes. I was reluctant to discard my uniform in case I was captured but that problem was solved when a jacket and trousers far too big for me were produced. These I was able to wear over my uniform and, although the weather was very warm, I felt much happier like that.

When the man who had questioned me returned later in the day he was accompanied by a younger man who, it was explained, would take me across the border on his bicycle. He pedalled hard, with me on his crossbar, and to this day I can remember him panting in my left ear. Much of the way was through quiet country lanes but then we dismounted and followed a footpath along a hillside. Looking down we could see armed soldiers at the border, on the road below. Eventually we were able to remount the cycle and continue until we reached a wood and then had to walk again. Eventually we reached a woodsman's hut and I was told that I was to remain there in hiding until someone came for me next day. With food and drink to last about twenty four hours I settled down in the bare hut. Even though I had on two layers of clothing I was cold and the floor was hard, so I didn't sleep much. Just after daybreak I heard vehicles moving quite close by and curiosity soon got the better of me. Soon after leaving the hut I saw German army lorries moving along a road. This was my first real sight of the enemy close to, and I was well within cover of the trees, but I soon returned to the cover of the hut.

I felt lonely and the waiting seemed interminable until eventually, some time in the afternoon, I heard someone approaching and the door was pushed open. A man entered and greeted me with a handshake, explaining that he would be taking me into Beauring, a small Belgian town in the Ardennes, where I would meet another member of the Resistance. We could not be seen together. He walked some distance ahead of me pushing his bicycle with its rear tyre deflated. Being a warm Sunday afternoon, some of the occupants of houses along the cobbled street were sitting outside in the sunshine. I felt very exposed but, apart from the occasional "Bonjour" to which I nodded in response, no-one appeared to pay much attention to me, much to my relief. When my guide with the bicycle turned left into an unpaved tree-lined road I followed him and was soon intercepted by another man who I was to get to know very well.

Roger Wautelet was a leader of Resistance Groupe 186 de la Legion Belge which, among its various activities, specialised in the repatriation of escaping aircrew. Roger took me to a small hamlet called Gozin, not far from Beauring, where his parents had a farm. The farm buildings were around a large courtyard and I was hidden in a small room above a barn. It was reasonably comfortable, with a small table, two chairs and a bed. There was a small window and although I was warned to stay out of sight I could, with care, see much of the activity in and around the farm during daylight. Food was usually brought to me by a farm worker who I soon learned was in hiding himself. His name was Joseph Michielle, who came from Brussels and had worked at Bon Marche but had come to Gozin to avoid being taken to Germany as a foreign worker. He and I became good friends.

Sometimes I was taken to the house after dark, to listen to the BBC news, which was always preceded by the "di di di dah" of the "Victory V". In the parlour I met Roger's mother, father and his two young sisters, Marcelle and Marie Louise. Maybe it was my imagination but I never felt that they were at ease when I was present. I thought .that I saw fear in his mother's eyes, even though I feel sure that Roger would never have put his own family at risk. There were two or three other occasions when I accompanied Roger into Beauring at night, after curfew. We visited an auberge and had drinks with the owner, Madame Brach, and some of her friends. I learned that her husband had been a Resistant, had been arrested by the Germans and was in a concentration camp. On one occasion as we were returning from Beauring and watching out for the lights of German vehicles, we could hear the sounds of a bomber stream passing overhead on its way to Germany. There were sounds of gunfire and then the clouds above lit up as an aircraft was hit. It plunged in flames to crash a few miles away with a tremendous noise. Everything happened so quickly we thought that no-one could have survived but, about a week later, I met the aircraft navigator, Roy Evans. He had bailed out and was being helped by the same resistance group as myself.

We met at a house in Beauring, where I also met Nippy Knight, who had previously been to visit me in my hiding place. Nippy was an Engineer Leader and had been in hiding in the area for some time. On this occasion we had all been brought together because apparently there was a plan to fly us home, an SOE operation I supposed. We stayed together in the house, feeling somewhat elated until, in the small hours of the morning, we were told that the operation had been aborted because of night-fighter activity at the nearby airbase at Florennes. We parted company that night and I never saw either of them again.

After being returned to my hiding place it was some time before I bade farewell to the Wautelet family and was again taken by Roger to the House in Beauring.. Soon after dawn we went by car to a cross roads in the country where I said goodbye to Roger Wautelet, a good friend to whom I owed so much. Not long after that he was captured and taken to Germany where, after suffering hunger and torture, he paid with his life at the extermination camp of Ellrich. At the crossroads I was picked up by another car containing two people, both armed, and driven to Namur. There I stayed for two nights in a house with two ladies who, to me as a nineteen year old, seemed quite elderly but probably were not.

On the third day of my stay a black Citroen car stopped outside. The driver came in and was introduced to me as Captain Jackson. As we shook hands I noticed that the little finger of his right hand was missing, but then thought no more about it. When he said that he would be taking me to Brussels I accepted without question, having by this time complete faith in all those who were helping me to return to England. I thanked the two ladies for their hospitality and help and said goodbye. In the car I was introduced to a well dressed lady, probably in her early forties, who was wearing a Red Cross badge on her jacket. We travelled about seventy kilometres to Brussels and I remember little about the journey.

Little did I realise that the man I thought was helping me to escape was none other than the notorious double agent Prosper Dezitter, alias The Captain, Jack Killane, or Herbert Call to name a few. He spoke English with a Canadian accent, claimed to be Canadian and to have lived in America for thirteen years, and said he was an officer of the British Secret Service. Apparently he had actually helped aircrew to escape through Spain in order to establish his credentials with the British authorities, although he had really been a member of the Gestapo since 1940 and specialised in the infiltration of escape organisations. The lady in the car, Annie, was not only his mistress but also an agent of the Gestapo and, like the Captain, had several aliases.

On arrival in the Brussels suburb of Wolughe the car stopped outside a large house, 369 l'Avenue Sleghers, which was to be my new home for a few days. Much to my delight there were three or four other aircrew there who, like myself, had been collected by the Captain whilst being assisted by a Resistance group. The house was well organised and could perhaps be described as a sort of transit camp for escaping aircrew. A plump middle-aged lady did the cooking and cleaning and there were also two men. One wore a dog collar, purporting to be a priest and Harry, a very large Dutchman, was the general factotum. We had complete confidence in these people, who all spoke English.

Preparations were made for the next part of our journey home, which would take us south into France. I was at last persuaded that I must discard my uniform and even my identity disks because, it was explained, we would be travelling to Paris by train as a group of students who could speak only Flemish. We had complete trust in the Captain when he took us into the centre of Brussels, all dressed in respectable civilian clothes. In the large department store, 'Le Bon Marche', we sat at a counter and had ice cream, purchased be the Captain, and then were taken in turn to a nearby photo booth to obtain photographs required for identity cards, which we would need when crossing the border. During this outing we saw many Germans in uniform, most of them officers, and I think we were all pleased when we returned to the relative safety of the house.

When the day of departure arrived we boarded the train for Paris at the Gare du Midi. There were five of us accompanied by an interpreter and, although we had a compartment to ourselves, we were warned not to speak English, even to each other. Our guide and interpreter sat by the carriage door. When, at the border, French and German officials came on board, he collected all our documents and took them into the corridor for inspection. Later he took us to the dining car for a meal. Sitting in close company with German officers, none of us spoke, letting him order our food.

When we disembarked from the train at the Gare du Nord in Paris we had some difficulty in following the guide because the platform was crowded with German soldiers disembarking from another train. At the main exit he was met by another man, to whom he handed the leather document case that he had carried throughout the journey. We had been advised that this would happen and that we should then follow the new guide. This we did, walking along the main boulevard not as a group but in ones and twos at a reasonable distance. After a while the guide paused and, after looking back to check that none of us had gone missing, he then entered the doorway of a small hotel. We all followed him.

In the reception lobby the guide disappeared. As soon as the last member of our group entered we were surrounded by men with guns pointing at us demanding that we put up our hands. An air gunner called Sparrow was slow to obey and was pistol whipped to the ground. We had been betrayed!

I have since learned that our reception committee consisted of members of the Nazi SD (Sicherheitdienst) of the SS (Schuultzstaffel), all callous, brutal, and dedicated Nazis. We were handcuffed and taken out to a small bus which took us through Paris to the notorious prison at Fresnes. This prison was built in the 1890's, when Fresnes was a small village about ten kilometres south of Paris, and it became the largest prison in Europe. Fresnes was now a suburb of Paris and the Germans occupied it in September 1940, using it throughout the war to imprison, interrogate, torture and sometimes execute members of the Resistance. Captured members of the British SOE were also imprisoned there, including Odette Sansom (Churchill) who suffered dreadful physical torture there before being taken to a concentration camp.

The bus took us through the large entrance gates and across a courtyard to the administration block. I was made to strip and take a cold shower, then given back my underwear and my shoes with the laces removed, plus a khaki-coloured greatcoat smelling strongly of disinfectant and which was to be the only outer garment I had to wear during my stay in Fresnes. Then I was taken to the cell block, which was a large hall with iron steps leading up to a number of iron catwalk-style galleries and along which were rows of solid steel cell doors. In each door there was a peephole and a port measuring about ten inches by six inches through which our food was passed. My cell was about twelve feet long by six feet wide and nine feet high and in the far wall was a heavily barred translucent window, about five feet high and three feet wide. The transom opening at the top was quite beyond reach. To the left of the cell door was a toilet without a seat and a wash basin with a cold water tap. Against the wall was an iron bedstead and above it was a bare electric light bulb that could be switched on and off only by guards outside the cell. On the walls were crude calendars scratched there by previous inmates to mark the duration of their stay, or possibly to count days before their execution.

My reaction to being imprisoned in this awful place was a feeling of utter loneliness, fearful apprehension and helplessness bordering on despair. For the first time in my young life I had no-one to turn to for help or advice or to share my feelings with.

Breakfast consisted of a bitter-tasting brew that they called coffee; I believe it was made with acorns. This was ladled into my food bowl through the port in the door, but it was hot and there was also a piece of black bread, which I was informed contained sawdust. The midday meal consisted of a brown liquid containing some vegetable matter (soup?) and a slice of black bread. Once a week prisoners were taken outside for exercise in separate enclosures measuring twelve feet by three feet, each surrounded by ten feet high walls. On a number of occasions I was taken for interrogation. While waiting, prisoners were put into what seemed like cupboards where there was just enough room to stand in total darkness, which made it very intimidating. Interrogation, conducted by the Gestapo, invariably followed the same pattern:- "Where have you been hiding?", "Who were the people who helped you?" and "How did you get to Paris?". This last question was obviously just bluff because they had obviously been fully informed by their agent, the Captain. At the end of each interrogation came a threat and it was then that I bitterly regretted having given up my identity discs or "dog tags" as the Germans euphemistically called them. Without those to prove one's identity it permitted the Gestapo to treat an RAF evader as a spy or enemy agent.
"You tell us that you are in the RAF and that you were shot down but, if that is so, where are your 'dog-tags'? All servicemen have them so why have you not got yours? You were caught wearing civilian clothes and carrying false identity papers and you know that, unless you answer our questions, we can have you shot as an enemy agent." I would then be returned to my solitary cell, to brood on the future, if I had any!

One morning during my second week in captivity hope did arise. My cell door was opened to admit, to my surprise and (almost) elation, a Luftwaffe officer. He looked immaculate, in the way that German officers often did and I, still with a minimum of clothing and that awful ill-fitting khaki greatcoat, felt terribly inferior. All part of the psychology, no doubt. However, he saluted and greeted me with "Good morning sir.", then suggested that I should sit down. His job, he said, was to visit prisons in France looking for RAF aircrew. Then he explained that my situation, being in Gestapo custody and without means of identity, was extremely perilous, inferring that he had my best interests at heart and that, if I answered his questions, he could secure my release from the Gestapo and Fresnes. The Luftwaffe wanted to do for RAF aircrew what they would hope would be done for their own aircrew who might find themselves in similar circumstances to mine. I reminded him that he must be aware that I could only tell him my name, rank, and number but he insisted that, if he was to secure my release, it would be necessary for me to help him convince the Gestapo that I was who I claimed to be. So the questioning continued until he eventually said that, if I could not be co-operative, there was no point in continuing the dialogue. When he suggested that I should think very carefully about my precarious situation I told him that I was very much aware of it. Then, in desperation, I appealed to him to verify the shooting down of an RAF bomber if I told him the date, time, and general area of our shooting down. That, I thought, would not be giving away any secrets and, if there were other survivors who might now be in captivity, that should enable him to establish my identity. When he departed he gave me no reason for optimism.

A few days later he returned to continue the questioning but then again left without making any promises about my future. However, shortly after that I was taken from my cell to shower and then given a uniform to wear. The uniform was khaki with gilt buttons and may have been American. Together with three other RAF aircrew I was taken to the railway station by armed guards from the Luftwaffe, who accompanied us to Frankfurt and on to Dulag Luft, the Luftwaffe interrogation centre for aircrew. When we arrived at Frankfurt, which had frequently been a target for Bomber Command, we were surrounded on the platform by angry civilians, but our guards kept them away from us.

Two and a half months after being "reported missing" I arrived at Dulag Luft and became an official prisoner of war. After more interrogation many of us were put into freight cars to travel in cold and uncomfortable conditions for several days and nights until we eventually arrived in Lithuania. There we were imprisoned in Stalag Luft VI, Heydekruge. It was no fun being a prisoner but we were all lucky to be alive and for me, in particular, it was now a shared experience. After Fresnes, nothing could ever be that bad again.

(As Shakespeare might have said "He seduced me with honest trifles, to betray me later in deepest consequence" Editor)

Equipage allemande de la 2ème escadrille du I./NJG 4:

Pilote....:lieutenant Wilhelm SCHNEIDEWIND (né le 24-7-1.912)
Radio.....:sergent Oswin MENHERT (né le 14-7-1.920)
Mitrailleur:sergent Werner UHLMANN (né le 28-6-1.920)

German Gunners Logbook Entry B.F.110

lfd. Nr. des Fluges	Führer	Begleiter	Muster	Zulassungs- Nr.	Zweck des Fluges	Abflug Ort
49 11	R. Schneidewind	Lest. Uff. Menner	Bf 110	C3+KK	Einsatz+J	Florennes
50	„	„	Bf 110	C3+CK	Überführung	„
51	„	„	Bf 110	C3+CK	„	„
52	„	„	Bf 110	C3+DK	„	„
53 12	„	„	Bf 110	C3+CK	Einsatz	„
54	„	„	Bf 110	C3+CK	Überführung	„
55	„	„	Bf 110	C3+CK	Einsatzflug	Melo
56	„	„	Bf 110	C3+CK	Nachtjagd	Florennes
57	„	„	Bf 110	C3+CK	Einsatzflug	St. Dizier
58 13	„	„	Bf 110	C3+CK	Einsatz	Florennes
59 14	„	„	Bf 110	C3+CK	Einsatz	„
60 15	„	„	Bf 110	C3+DK	„	„

Flugbuch

für

Werner Uhlmann

Werner UHLMANN

begonnen am: 13. 5. 1940.

beendet am: _____

Flug		Landung			Flug-	Kilometer	Bemerkungen
Tag	Tageszeit	Ort	Tag	Tageszeit	dauer		
15.7.43	02⁰⁰	Florennes	15.7.43	04⁰⁸	128'	768	Feind. 7A.
17.7.43	21⁴⁹	"	17.7.43	22¹⁵	16'	156	
25.7.43	21¹⁵	"	25.7.43	21³⁴	19'	114	
28.7.43	21⁵²	"	28.7.43	22¹⁴	22'	132	
30.7.43	23⁵⁵	"	31.7.43	01¹³	78'	468	Feind. 7B {2. Abschuss...}
2.8.43	21¹⁰	Venlo	2.8.43	21⁴⁷	37'	222	
3.8.43	19⁰⁰	Florennes	3.8.43	19⁴⁵	34'	204	Sehr scharf avion attaqué à 0h 47 avion abattu à 0h 48)
7.8.43	23³⁶	St. Dijier	8.8.43	00⁴⁴	42'	252	avion: Short Stirling, qui a ... (catastrophe et s'est ... en flamme.)
8.8.43	6³⁹	Florennes	8.8.43	07²¹	42'	252	
10.8.43	1⁰⁰	Florennes	10.8.43	1⁴²	42'	252	Stefan
10.8.43	23³⁴	"	11.8.43	2⁴¹	187'	1122	Feind 7B
12.8.43	23³⁶	"	13.8.43	2¹¹	155'	930	4.5
					9,24'	19228	

Lager Nr. 1395 E. Wützrig, Dahme-Mark

IT SEEMED A GOOD IDEA

By Bernard Smith

September 1943, Shellingford, Berks, 3 EFTS, Grading School. I am on guard duty, protecting the airfield from I know not what. It is 2 a.m. there is a moon and the night is very dark, cold and to add to our misery, it begins to drizzle, we have another two hours of this. My mate is a tall cheerful Irish man from Belfast. We are garbed for the night and prepared for any action, which means, we are wearing tin hat, greatcoat, balaclava, a present from my Aunt, gloves, scarf and large boots. We carry a rifle but no ammunition and a small pack. Con slides up to me and whispers in my ear, much as Eve might have done in the garden. His honeyed tones fall on my receptive ears. Says he "We don't have to suffer this perishing cold, or endure the tiresome process of walking." Alarm bells ring, I am wary, having heard such

Tiger Moth

seditious talk before and suffered the consequences. He leads me to a Tiger Moth two cockpits in tandem, with removable covers, parked inconspicuously amongst several others. Splendid thinks I, what a brilliant idea, foolproof. We climb in with rifle, settle down, pull the covers across and relax happily. My last words, a caution, "We must not go to sleep," "Not a chance says he".

My sleep is shattered by the aggravating racket of an engine coming to life, people are so inconsiderate. Half asleep, I ponder the situation, but not for long, a large gloved hand swept my hood back. It was daylight and I meet the startled gaze of Cadet Baines, who utters words of encouragement, "The whole camp is looking for you". The other face completely devoid of sympathy or humour was that of our Flight Commander, I shot out, and completely unnerved, Con so far undisturbed and unaware of our changed circumstances emerged, said "Good God its 8.30," and hastened to join us. It occurred to me that Con's, glib tongued that he undoubtedly was, would be pushed to talk us out of this one. Feeling distinctly overdressed, we ran the gauntlet of amused instructors and cheerful comrades offering dubious advice and unhelpful suggestions,

At the flight office we found that Sue, our corporal clerk had correctly assessed the situation and offered two cups of tea, and a kind smile. God bless her. The Guard Room were advised that we had materialised. We endured a verbal bashing from the C.O., who ended his tirade with words giving us food for thought, He said "You do realise, in time of war, you can be shot for deserting your post." I hoped he was joking. A very large, bad tempered, Sgt. of Police arrived to collect us. Fixing an angry eye on me, he said "Thanks to you I have missed my breakfast" seemed unwise to suggest we had missed ours. Arriving at the Guard Room, we were advised we were on a 'fizzer', which in English meant a charge. We stood miserably in front of our Commanding Officer, as his Warrant Officer read the charge. Says he "Well what have you got to say for yourselves?". Personally, I could think of nothing, having completely run out of ideas. Con likewise. He suggested our future in the RAF could be difficult if we failed to change our wicked ways. His verdict, "Guilty", 5 extra duties and fatigues, being our punishment. The Service Police were patently scandalised at such leniency and I couldn't believe our luck. I heard later from the clerk. The C.O. in an aside to his Adjutant, had said "A novel idea, shows initiative and imagination.

400 MPH - IN A LANCASTER!

By V Lambourne D.F.C

No.207 Squadron, Bottisford, Notts., Lancaster EM-K-5863. Target - Saarbrucken rail yards, on 9th July'42 take off 2355 hrs, no moon.

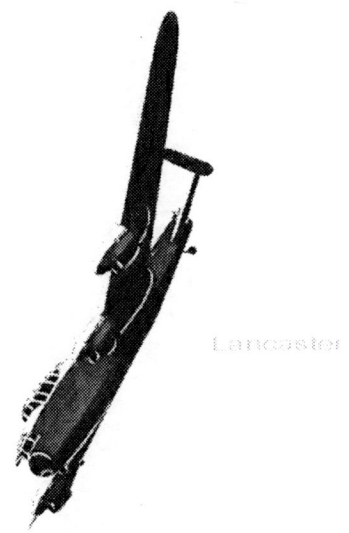

Only two aircraft were detailed to attack, and as we approached the target area, the moon came up to cause the rails in the sidings to shine brilliantly. We were flying at 15,000 ft, and observed one searchlight and one Flak gun busy with our other aircraft but no further opposition. My Pilot, (F/O Sharland) and the Bomb Aimer discussed the situation, and decided on a low level attack!. Being in the mid upper turret I watched our descent with some trepidation, as someone called out that we had a 4,000 pounder, and not to go too low!. Height was being called out and we levelled out at 4,500 feet, directly over a mass of trucks and containers. Our Bomb Aimer let go the entire load, the 4,000 bomb and 8 containers of incendiaries, then into a climbing turn to clear the area.

As we turned away, there was a brilliant flash from below, and our aircraft tipped up on to its nose, and began to dive; the flak battery had us in its sights, and shells were extremely close. Our nose dive, I heard later, was touching 400mph. With painful ears plus unable to move, I watched the rapidly approaching roofs and streets of Saarbrucken, awaiting oblivion, I think I called out "Oh no". Suddenly our nose started to rise up and a tremendous force was trying to shove me out of the turret, then with relief and amazement I saw in the grey light, trees, a lamp post, pavement and railings! the engines were screaming as we pulled out at approximately 100 feet!.

As we climbed away and set course for home, my Pilot said things were not normal as we had a drift to port, everything appeared in place as viewed from the mid upper turret however, we were still flying and made 1,200 ft. The rest of the flight was uneventful, luckily, landing at base at 05,30.

During breakfast the Station Engineering Officer came to us saying our Lanc. was in the hanger and come and take a look. As we entered the open hanger doors we all gasped, and could not believe our eyes, both wings had a cracked main spar beyond each inner engine, and the wings had super "droop" or anhedral. We were very lucky.

IFF OR NOT

By V Lambourne D.F.C

.No.12 Squadron, Wickenby, Linc's.1 Group. 11 June 1943. Take off for Dusseldorf 22.45 hrs.Lancaster W4380. PH-ETarget, City, 800 aircraft attacking in two waves, clear night with a moon. Bomb load 1 x 4000, 6 x 30 SBC's, 7 x 4 SBC's..

The flight outwards was quiet, peaceful, just the drone of the engines, and thinking what sort of Hell were we heading for, we were soon to find out !. The Target Indicator Markers were on time, and the searchlights plus Flak were busy. At this point I must tell you Air Ministry had ordered the sealing of I.F.F. controls, as German night fighters had been tracking us on the route home, and shooting us down, with their new type of AI equipment, locked on to our I.F.F. transmission frequency.

However, on the run in, at around 17,000 ft. vast fires covered half of the City, and the Flak was heavy. Searchlights, hundreds of them, were finding aircraft and holding them in a large cone of light, then the Flak got busy, heavy and light. We were on our level run for dropping, when a cloud of Flak burst around us, and searchlights began to gather, hundreds of silver discs looking up at us. As our bomb load left we dived to starboard to clear the light cone, but were held, and shell bursts getting closer and closer, also shell splinters rattling down the fuselage to the rear. My thoughts were "can I do anything", "but what", "we shall be shot down". Then I looked down to the I.F.F. panel, and thought, "there must be something", and reached for my leather gloves, put the right hand glove on, and smashed down the switches of the I.F.F. controls, the lead seals flew, and I watched the scene below.

 After a few seconds, to my amazement, the searchlights broke away, and with hundreds of others, around the city, started a series of uncontrolled gyrations; up and down circling the sky, some rotating, and lighting up the town, an amazing spectacle. The Flak had also ceased and as we pulled away at around 12,000ft in blissful darkness, began to realise that the radiated signal from my I.F.F. had jammed the German Radar control of both Searchlights and Flak Batteries. When we were a few miles from the target, I switched it OFF to prove it all, and sure enough, all the Flak started up and Searchlights rose up to search the sky. As we were in the first wave now turning home, I switched it all on, and again there was the total collapse of everything!!. I kept the I.F.F. on, as the second wave was coming in, leaving it on for at least 50 miles or so. We were at about 18,000ft after a careful climb, and I could see the target glow in the sky, but no searchlights.

Back at base I reported it all informing my Signals Officer, and Group, that German defence Radar was on or close to our I.F.F. frequency, on stud one. We had lost the Night Fighters, but gained something much better. 18 Flak holes were counted in all around the fuselage, but nothing vital was hit.

ONCE IS ENOUGH!

By V Lambourne D.F.C.

Early in 1939 I volunteered for the R.A.F.V.R. when Hitler was making a noise in Munich. I was educated at Oxford, which was also my home, and flew from Kidlington Aerodrome, where the Oxford University Air Squadron also trained; and with them was a certain gentleman, P/Officer Leonard Cheshire, of whom we all know much about!.

After my W/T courses at Cranwell and Hamble, Gunnery up in West Freugh, Scotland, I was posted to O.T.U. at Upper Heyford, Oxfordshire! what luck!!. Passing out from O.T.U. I found my name missing from the Ops' posting list, and was informed I was staying on as a Staff Radio Instructor!, what luck again (14 miles from home). (Ed.- sounds like a bloody fiddle to me). Hampden and Avro Anson aircraft dealt with all trades.

On the 15th of April 1941 the crew bus took us to Brackley Night Flying ground, where we took off on a long cross country at 19.45, Northampton - Bury St. Edmonds - Spalding - Horncastle and Brockley. Bright moonlight welcomed us as we came in to land on a grass and gooseneck flared runway. We passed the Chance light, and bounced somewhat higher than usual down the field I thought, and counted 12 flares in all, and the end was a red one! We were still bouncing and moving fast, so I shouted to my Wireless Operator pupil to ditch the guns and copula, which we did over the side, and lay on the floor. There as a very loud noise of crashing and splintering of timber, noticing branches of trees going in all directions, then a big bang as our starboard wing hit something solid, and I saw above, the top half of a telegraph pole with insulators and wires, pass away over us, ending up across a country road and into soft earth. We were both unhurt and leapt up and out down the fuselage which was close to the ground. I shouted to the pilot and navigator to get clear, which they did, and seeing a cottage some thirty yards away I set off and the crew followed, through lots of mangled cabbages etc.. As we got close to the cottage door, it suddenly opened, and standing there was an old gentleman in a long white night gown and cap, and holding up a storm lantern, saying "who are you lot, what was that awful noise", whereupon my pilot (P/O Hirons) explained over tea in the kitchen, that we had been on a night flying practice and had come through the hedge. I didn't say too much to him, and luckily he had a telephone, eventually the ambulance and Fire Brigade turned up, so we were taken to the Station Medical Officer for a check up and so to bed.

Two days later we took off from Brackley with P/O Caldwell, in a Hampden P850, on a cross country at 20.00hrs. The route was much the same as on the 15th. Coming in to land around midnight, there was still a good moon and a clear night. We touched down by the side of the Chance light and sailed down the line of gooseneck flares, and it was not until I saw the red one go past, that I realised we were still 70% airborne. I said to myself "Oh no, it can't be", and yelled to my Wireless Operator pupil to "heave the guns out and the Cupola", that done we both lay on the floor. There was an unearthly crash and deceleration as our undercarriage left us and we then came to a grinding halt. Smelling petrol I shouted "Get out", and we found ourselves in soft soil of a garden. Then I noticed the white painted Thatched Farm House.

The crew were all out and I said "Over here" and we all made for the house door. I had been here before. The door suddenly opened, and standing there in night shirt and cap, holding a storm lantern, was the old gent, who lifted the lantern, looked at me and said "My God not you again!!". The rest you know, with tea and biscuits.

WATER WATER EVERYWHERE - BUT

By Wg. Cdr A.W.L. "Paddy" Mahon

In May 1939 No. 228 Squadron, equipped with Sunderland flying boats, were sent on extended detached duty from Pembroke Dock to Alexandria to attend major Fleet exercises in the Eastern Mediterranean. The Squadron was accommodated aboard a specially adapted elderly British India liner the "Dumana". The Officers were in the First Class, the senior N.C.O.'s in the Second Class and the rest of the Squadron were in very substandard, almost squalid "Troopship" accommodation.

Arrangements had been made with Imperial Airways for the use of their slipway for taking our aircraft out of the water for the 60 hour inspections, which could not be carried out afloat, including the washing out of the bilge's and the hosing down of the hull with fresh water. It was decided that the charges being made for the use of fresh water were excessive and that an alternative be sought. The first solution tried was for the aircraft to be flown as they become due, to the Sea of Galilee, known to be of fresh water. The trip was treated as a nav-ex departing Alexandria at first light. The landing at Galilee was invariably interesting, into the sun on a dead calm whilst the altimeter passed through zero when the aircraft was still 600 feet above the water! The whole of the rest of the day was spent in carrying out the 60 hour inspection and the washing of the hull and the bilge's. Fortunately the APU was well adapted to the hosing down and the subsequent pumping of the bilge's.

Time was given for the crews, which were supplemented with the tradesman not normally part of the crew, to have welcome swims. An overnight stop gave everybody a chance to dry out and the following morning the aircraft was flown to Cyprus landing at Famagusta. On this part of the trip it was usual to pick up some members of the Palestine Police Force who saved a couple of days of their leave time in Egypt. The rest of that day and the daylight hours of the following day were considered a "Make & Mend", (Standown to landlubbers). Take off at dusk, night flight to and a night landing at Aboukir completed the exercise.

These trips were found to be expensive in flying hours so a second scheme was sought. The Squadron Commander, Wg. Cdr Kelly Barnes, later to be interned In Iceland in peculiar circumstances, decided to recce.. Lake Quarun, some 110 miles SSE of Alexandria. On the 27th July he flew to the lake and carried out a very short landing. The lake was quite shallow in places and fortunately the bottom was thick mud. Taxiing around using a lead line he found a reasonable anchorage about 300 yards offshore close to a village, he also found that the lake was extremely salty! Having had lunch and deciding that the lake could be considered only as an emergency landing area he started the outer engines, retrieved the anchor and taxied out towards the centre of the lake. But on starting the starboard inner the engine caught fire and the rear cover was badly damaged before the fire was extinguished. The boat was taxied back to the original anchorage and a message passed by WT to the Base ship.

One aircraft was despatched to the Lake with extra rations and fresh water for the stranded crew and to return the C.O. to the "Dumana". The aircraft on which I was co-pilot to Pit. Off Laurie Ellis, was readied to transport a spare engine, a task we had previously carried out. To accommodate the engine a large V-shaped panel had to he removed from the port side of the hull immediately under the bomb-bay hatch. The engine, on its wooden transit case, was brought to the aircraft on a bomb scow, a flat topped shallow craft fitted with two engines for ease of manoeuvring, an asset when handling an awkward load between hull and wing tip float. Our normal bomb winch and carriage were used to lift the engine inboard and it was soon located and secured to specially provided pads on the main keelsons of the hull. The side panel was re-secured by its 100 odd quarter inch bolts, rations were taken aboard for four days for our crew plus the Sergeant fitter and the extra engine mech. who were to assist the normal crews, most of whom, including myself, were tradesmen. All this had taken most of the day but we decided that we could make the Lake before dusk. This we did and having been given landing directions from the other boats we landed and dropped our anchor upwind of the "lame duck", thinking it would help when we came to transferring the engine. The relief aircraft took off with the C.O. aboard and the remaining crews went into a huddle to discuss the best way to carry out our job. We decided on the need for two platforms able to carry an engine each and one for the propeller which had to be accommodated whilst the engines were changed over. Our transport between boats was by use of the large dinghies carried by each boat, unfortunately they had to be rowed everywhere, we'd have given our eye teeth for that ugly bomb scow! By now it was dark and we turned in for an early start.

After breakfast produced by our priceless airframe mech., both dinghies set off for the village with three officers and two NCO`s. A few days previous to this trip I had badly scalded my left leg and the M.O had let me go on the trip if I agreed to keep it scrupulously clean. So when the dinghies grounded on the mud some yards from the shoreline the party rallied round to bear me to dry land. The village headman who had come down to meet us decided that must make me the boss man and he would only talk to me. Fortunately he had a smattering of English and I had the merest touch of Arabic so we got it straightened out. Between all of us we arranged for the hire of some eight very cranky canoes and some timber with which to construct the three rafts, using three canoes for each engine raft and two for the propeller. Whilst this was going on the crews were busy getting the propeller ready for lifting off and the raft for the task, being first made, was poled and sculled out to the aircraft. By now the temperature had soared and it was agreed that work should cease until later in the day. We had rigged the awnings that were part of the aircraft equipment but they didn't extend to the inner engines, any metal outside their shade soon became hot enough to burn bare skin. To prove a point our rigger fried an egg on top of the hull not shaded by the awning. We adopted this siesta for the rest of our stay.

It was about this time that we realised that with virtually no current flow the effluent from our flushing toilet was not dispersing and it was decided that operations of that sort had to be carried out some distance from the aircraft. One was required to don an inflated Mae West, arm oneself with a tablet of sea water soap and paddle to some distance before functioning. We had only one instance when the wearer forgot to tightly fasten the lower strap of his Mae West.

Paddy circling buoy

The rest of day two was spent in the final removal of the propeller, using the winch and gantry carried on each aircraft and which was secured above the engine nacelle. The prop was secured on to the smaller platform and we attempted to move it to the aircraft but the breeze which had sprung up bore it shore wards and we allowed it to ground and secured it for the night.

Day three saw the arrival of a Sunderland bearing more fresh water in barrels borrowed from "Dumana's" lifeboats. We started on the removal of the damaged engine and lifted out the replacement engine onto its improvised platform. After a few "hairy" attempts to achieve a reasonable balance we started on the journey between the aircraft learning much about the problems of navigating it. We finally moored it alongside the lame duck and helped with the lowering of the damaged engine onto the second platform. Once that was secure we took it back to our aircraft and readied it for stowage in the bomb compartment. The rest of the engine trades hauled the replacement engine under the nacelle and hoisted it into its location and started the installation sequence. By dusk both engines were secure and the propeller had been recovered and fitted.

Day 4 saw the final adjustments and the first of two engine tests. It must be appreciated that for each run the outer engines had to be started, the anchor recovered and the reverse on completion of the run. No running up on the chocks! The second run proved successful and shortly after the aircraft took off for Alexandria. Our crew returned the platforms to the village and said our farewells to the Arabs who had been very helpful, in return for which we had regaled them with coffee and cigarettes during our enforced siestas.

We were airborne in the late afternoon on our way to the Imperial Airways base on the Nile near Cairo, ready for the night off amid the fleshpots that the C.O. had promised us. As a footnote to this experience, the crews had refused to treat me to my special status after that first day, and I had to take my chance with the mud and salty water. On my return to "Dumana" the M.O. found my leg had healed without scarring. He suggested that we return to the Lake and bring back a few barrels of the mud for sale at "a guinea a box".

SUNDERLAND PILOT

A very young Sergeant Pilot had to fly a Sunderland flying boat from the Thames estuary down to Cornwall. He was joined at the last moment by an Air Commodore from Air Ministry, London. As soon as they were airborne, the Air Commodore who hadn't flown a plane for 25 years since crashing an SE5A in 1917 near Ypres said "OK Sergeant I'll take over now" and proceeded to struggle and fight the controls all over the sky. The Sgt pilot, although officially responsible for the aircraft wasn't going to assert his authority with such a high ranking officer, sat there petrified but somehow navigated the Sunderland down to Cornwall.

The Air Commodore made a terrible approach to the runway and was just

about to touch down when a desperate Sgt somehow found his voice at last and said "Excuse me Sir, but do you realise this is a seaplane and can't land on an airfield?" The Gold Braid from Air Ministry rammed all four throttles forward, missed the Control Tower by inches, flew to the nearest bay, bounced in for a very heavy landing, swung round on his petrified companion saying "Damn it Sgt, you don't think I was really going to land on an airfield, do you?" and stepped off into the water.

"FLY AND DELIVER" A FERRY PILOT'S STORY

By Alan Greaves

When the war ended I was a pilot on a Beaufighter squadron in Athens, where we had been sent to help the Greek government prevent the Communists from taking over. In 1946, as a Warrant Officer, I was offered a commission if I would sign on for a year after my demob. date. Not particularly keen to return to an uncertain future on civvy street, I accepted and was posted back to the U.K in 1946, after nearly four years away.

Following a spot of leave I was posted to No 1 Ferry Unit, RAF Pershore, Worcestershire, in November 1946. The Winter of 46/47 was one of the coldest on record, and RAF Pershore must have been one of the coldest spots in England, especially to one used to living in Africa and the Middle East for the past few years. I was therefore pleased when I was instructed to take a Beaufighter Mk 10 to Negombo, Ceylon. The route we planned was via Bordeaux, Istres, Luqa, Malta, Heliopolis, Cairo, Shaiba, Karachi, Poona and Ceylon. AS this involved some rather long legs, beyond the normal range of the Beau, the aircraft was fitted with a long range fuel tank under the belly, rather like a torpedo.

We took off early on 5th December and just about on the point of lift-off, there was a resounding "bang" and the aircraft shook violently. Anyway, I completed the take-off, retracted the undercarriage, trimmed the plane, checked the instruments and asked my navigator if he could see anything wrong. All seemed to be OK so I called up the tower who told me they thought that my port tyre had burst on take-off. I was instructed to lower the undercarriage and make a low-level pass in front of the tower. This I did and the tower confirmed that indeed my port tyre was in tatters and that I should circle the field for further instructions. These were to jettison the fuel in the long range tank and most of it in the normal tanks, and then drop the tank on the field.

As I was jettisoning the fuel, I thought of how many miles I could have driven with it on my 350cc Rudge motorcycle, it must have been about five years petrol ration! My next job was to jettison the long range fuel tank. This was rather like launching a torpedo, so I flew low over the field, pressed the button and voila! The tank went bouncing down the field, through a fence at the end, into a farmer's field and ended up in the farmer's hut. Luckily no one was in it at the time. The tower then told me I had two choices: I could either make a wheels up belly landing or try to make a normal landing, favouring the starboard wheel and hope that the undercarriage didn't collapse. I consulted my navigator and we both agreed that the latter was the best option.

The tower was told of my decision and they gave me clearance to make the approach, using the grass rather than the runway. On the final it was a bit off-putting to see the blood wagon and the fire engine following me down the runway. Anyway I managed to make a decent landing, holding off on the right wheel until the last minute and dropping the left damaged one as gently as possible. Not wanting to use the brakes too heavily, I rolled to a gentle stop with only a slight swing to port and came to a stop without any damage, much to our relief.

After a relatively quiet night in the mess we were given another plane and started all over again on December 6th. The flights via our planned routes were uneventful until we were approaching Poona. Flying over the high hills I saw something on our left quarter coming rapidly towards me, I tried to bank to starboard but too late. A large vulture struck my port engine and made a nasty mess of both it and himself. I throttled the engine back and called up Poona tower and was told to make an immediate emergency landing.

At times like this I felt sorry for the poor old navigator, sitting aft in his little bubble and not really knowing what was going on. Again I was lucky in that the damage wasn't too bad and I was able to land without any problem.

As the plane would take a while to repair, and as it was getting near Christmas, we were delighted to be told that we could return to the U.K. This involved a train to Bombay, a TATA airline flight to Karachi and then a BOAC Sandringham flying-boat Karach-Bahrein-Basra Cairo-Augusta (Sicily)--Marignan (France)- Poole. What luxury! My first experience on a civil aircraft and no night flying, so wonderful stops in luxurious hotels on the way. Little did I think then that I would eventually join BOAC and spend twenty-six years with them and British Airways.

This isn't the end of the story, however, as another crew were sent to Poona to fly on the repaired Beau. Sadly, both engines cut on take-off and the crew were both killed. The Gods were looking after me! I had many more interesting ferry trips including one delivering a Fairchild Argus to a US Airforce Major, ex B17 pilot, in Paris. He'd bought it through the PX!. But that's another story.

A REMARKABLE STORY

By Kevin Muncer

Flying Officer Kevin Muncer considers himself a very lucky man as the following true story will reveal: the date was March 16th. 1945. Having completed a bombing raid on Nurnberg the 166 Squadron Lancaster based at Kirmington, Lincs. was homeward bound when suddenly all hell broke loose and 24 year old pilot Muncer's aircraft was severely damaged by enemy fighter fire. Kevin, with his left arm shattered above the elbow, was being thrown around the cockpit of the plummeting plane. He thought his young life was about to end. With a resounding crash his head hit the perspex canopy, normally capable of supporting the weight of a man, with such force that a hole was created through which he was able to struggle, and with his other arm pull the ripcord of his parachute.

Almost as soon as he touched the ground he blacked out. He regained consciousness to find himself in a field and there was a strange lady applying a tourniquet to what remained of his mangled arm. This "angel of mercy" was in fact a German farmers wife who had seen the stricken airman parachuting to earth. Without thought of his being friend or foe she determined the only hope of saving his life before summoning medical help was to stem the flow of blood. Kevin's life had been saved but his problems were far from over.

He was transported to Bruckberg Military Hospital where, on March 17th, St. Patricks Day, his left arm was amputated at the shoulder; hardly the luck of the Irish one might think. Luck however was still on Kevin's side as a few days later the local militia arrived to demand his arrest and trial as a war criminal for the devastation the bombing had wreaked on the civilian population of Nurnberg. The Commanding Officer of the hospital, a WW1 Prussian veteran of the old school insisted he be treated as a prisoner of war and refused to release him. An armed guard was even placed on his ward to prevent his abduction by the angry locals. Some six weeks later he was freed from the hospital by the arrival of the advancing US Army.

Convalescing back in England, Kevin received a letter from the Red Cross seeking his help on behalf of one Frau Meyer, the "angel of mercy" from the farm in Wensdorf. Would he petition the War Office to hasten the release of her son a POW in Scotland, whose help was desperately needed on the farm which was struggling to survive in post war Germany. To quote Kevin, "the War Office responded with unusual speed and efficiency and within a week Frau Meyer had her son back on the farm".

The final chapter of this amazing saga concerns the watch, a gift from his sister, which Kevin was wearing on his left wrist at the time he lost his arm in the crashing Lancaster above the fields of Germany. A French P.O.W working in the fields came across the remains of Kevin's arm upon which was the watch. With commendable honesty Leon Planade gave the watch to the Red Cross, who identified it as Kevin's from his service number engraved on the casing.

Kevin Muncer D.F.C, now a robust 78 year old lives on the Kentish coast. The loss of an arm dosn`t prevent him from being a fierce competitor on the golf course or hoisting the occasional pint of his favourite beer. In 1984 he and his family visited Germany and enjoyed an emotional reunion with the Meyers.

COCONUTS, PALM OLIVES, AND MONEY

By Peter Crouch

By 1960 I had completed twelve years in Training Command and was currently instructing on the Vampire T11, I also had a Chipmunk T10 on my charge which was used for communication duties and 'jollies' The 'Posters' caught up with me at last however and I was posted to Singapore as a Transport Operations Officer at RAF Changi. Mary, Brian and I embarked on the Troopship Navasa for our journey to Singapore and on a wet and windy afternoon in February we slipped down the Solent for a rough crossing of 'The Bay'. There were many white faces aboard for a while but it was better when we entered the Med. We popped in to Gibraltar, Malta, Suez, where we waited for the convoy to form up and then we led them through the Suez Canal, this was the most fascinating part of the 'cruise'. Then it was Aden, Colombo and after three weeks we arrived in Singapore much to everyone's relief. Three weeks on a troop ship is definitely not a relaxing pleasure cruise. It was March the 21st and if you stood a pencil on its end it would cast no shadow because the sun was directly overhead. It was hot, humid and Singapore Harbour did not smell too sweet.

As a Transport Operation Officer I was a shift worker, a day shift, a night shift then two days off. You can get into a lot of trouble in Singapore if you have two days off out of every four so Mary and I took ourselves off to the local flying club and offered my services as an instructor. They were a bit cool to start with but when I told them I had been a basic instructor in the RAF and could fly the Chipmunk they helped me to get my Singapore Private Pilots Licence, and a Radio Telephony licence, and after I was checked out by the Chief Flying Instructor (CFI) I was accepted.

The Royal Singapore Flying Club had five aeroplanes, two Cessna 172's, a Cessna 150, a Chipmunk and a Tiger Moth. It had just lost its Government subsidy and was in financial difficulty. The club belonged to the members but the financial worries were not my concern, all I was interested in was the flying. We had many different nationalities in our membership list, too many to quote, but it was predominantly British. It was interesting to fly out of an International Airport being used by Dakotas, Fokker Friendships, Boeing 707's and other types of 'big jets' and we often had to hold off for one of them to make an approach and landing.

I was asked by the CFI if I would do a pay drop, I didn't know what a pay drop was but it sounded interesting. He explained that if you were a university graduate in Singapore you either worked as a civil servant or became a bandit, the communist confrontation was still active and there were still bandits around making it difficult to get the pay roll to the coconut and palm olive estates. It required an armoured van with twelve armed guards and took two days to get the money there until some one had the bright idea of delivering the money by air using the flying club aircraft. It was also a very useful form of income for the club.

"Just put down a bit of flap, get back to 60 knots" the CFI said "Run over the Padang (sports field) they will have put out a white cross, and let it go, take some one with you, you can't do it on your own. By the way they will probably be standing on the cross" and with that he walked off. I turned to Mary and said "Corporal, you are elected to drop the money" and between us we loaded the Cessna 172 with three sacks of money, containing about a million dollars, all double bagged in stout canvas sacks about two feet long and two feet in circumference. They must have weighed about forty pounds each.

Thinks.....a million dollars.....hmmmmm...where can you go from Singapore in a Cessna 172 and not get caught - no where really and I would have to split with Mary!

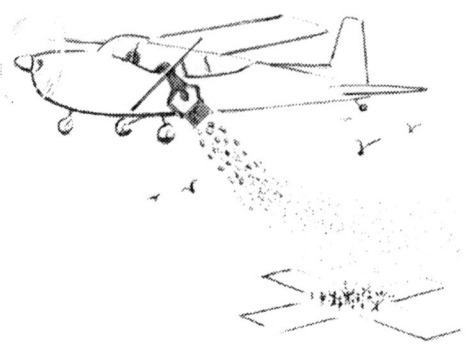

We took off and headed up into Malaya. After flying for about an hour we came to the palm olive estate where the money was to be dropped and circled the Administrative Centre and sure enough there was a white cross in the middle of the Padang and there was the reception committee, all four of them standing right in the middle of the cross! I plotted my run-in so that I would miss them and told Mary to take the bolt out of the window knuckle joint and let the window up under the wing and bring the first bag over without clobbering me. She did this quite well and then lowered the bag out of the window so that it was resting on the step just above the undercarriage wheel fairing. With a couple of miles to run to the drop I selected 'Take Off' flap and brought the speed back to sixty knots and as we came up level with the cross I shouted "Red On, Green On, Go" and Mary gave the bag a push and away it went. We didn't hit any one but it was close!. I applied full power and pulled the aircraft round in a turn to position for the next drop shouting to Mary to get Bag number two over and in position. By now I was pulling perhaps two "G" so the bag had an apparent weight of eighty pounds and Mary was having problems and was not happy! I made up my mind that after we had landed and I had a post flight beer in my hand I would explain the effects of "G" to her. As I straightened out of course the forces on the bag returned to normal and she had no further problems. The next two drops went off well and after a low pass and a wave we were on our way back to Singapore.

The Club was well paid for these drops, for the pilots it was free flying and it was fun. We were given an allowance of 2S$ (Singapore Dollars) for every flying hour, just the price of a bottle of beer!. I understand the Club was insured against the money being dropped in error. Thinks.....1,000,000 dollars, there must be some way I can make off with it and not get caught, but where and how?

I was a little suspicious when the CFI came and said he had received a phone call from a company that wanted money delivered to a small airfield way up in Northern Malaya. The company ran an iron ore mine called Bukit Besi (Iron Hill) and I estimated that it would take two and three quarter hours to get there, routing up the East coast of Malaya and mostly over jungle. There was also the monsoon weather to consider but avarice got the better of us and a few days later the CFI and I fired up a Cessna 150 and made the first flight. Navigation was easy, we just followed the coast most of the way and arrived at the small strip carved out of the jungle swamp. The resident engineers, mainly Brits and Aussies, were delighted to see us as visitors from outside the mine were few and far between. They took us to their Mess and started to fill us with beer so we had a quick conference and decided to night stop. It was a very quiet flight down to Singapore the next day.

It was at this point that the CFI asked me to be his deputy, I was not very keen in getting involved and said no, but he pressed and as he was such a nice chap I reluctantly said yes. He resigned the following day, the rotten swine, and I became the CFI.

We flew to the mine every other Thursday with the pay-roll, I did most of the flights over the next two years, we even started to teach a few of the engineers to fly but it was inevitable that some one would land in the marshy undershoot. The student was bruised but not badly so, the aeroplane was bent and had to be put on a lorry for the trip back to Singapore.

I never did figure out how to hijack the pay-roll but by this time I had completed my tour in Singapore and had been nominated for a captains course on the Argosy turbo prop transport starting in late 1962. The Club made Mary and I Life Members and as the British Eagle Britannia lifted off from Singapore bound for London I looked out and saw the Club buildings and the aircraft parked outside and realised what a wonderful two and a half years it had been and with regret, the good friends we were leaving behind.

MY FIRST TASTE OF A JET

By Peter Crouch

My aviation life had been pretty mundane, Whitleys, Halifaxes, Hastings, Ansons but the first two had a glider attached to them now and then, and there was nothing mundane about that, it was frightening at times! The last two years, beginning January 1949 had seen me flying the Anson 21 out of Hullavington with Navigators under training. This mark of Anson had hydraulics to retract the undercarriage and was a vast improvement on the original model. We flew Grimsby - Wrexham - Base day after day, night after night and when we complained of boredom they made it Wrexham - Grimsby - Base. That's navigator humour!

The Training Command 'Trappers' (examiners) paid us periodic visits during which I had to demonstrate my flying ability. Late in 1950 one of them said "You seem to have been here some time, where are you going to be posted to?". I had to confess that I didn't know what openings there were for a Flight Sergeant Pilot with just under two thousand hours. "The Central Flying School, Flight Sergeant, that is where you should go, become a flying instructor" he said " I will fix it" I said a very doubtful "Thank you Sir" wondering what I had let myself in for and would I not have been better to go as a Link Trainer Instructor or Target Towing!

Things moved pretty fast, the next thing I knew I was at RAF Little Rissington for an interview which I presume I passed because I was off to RAF Oakington for a single engine refresher course on Harvards. I remember my first slow roll, I lost 5,000 feet, but I did get better by the end of the course. Having been refreshed and given one landing from the back seat of the Harvard (which nearly caused me to AWOL - Absent Without

Leave) I went back to RAF Little Risington to join Course number 123 starting 1st January 1951.

Mary and I lived in a caravan and I was lucky enough to get a parking site behind the local pub where they sold an intoxicating brew called Yankee Bitter. It was a gill of Best Bitter and a gill of rough cider. The course lasted six months and to begin with I could manage a half, maybe a pint of this potent brew but by the end of the course I could drink two pints before anaesthesia took over. I graduated as a below average instructor but my ability on the dart board was rated as above average and occasionally exceptional depending how much I drank.

As students we were lectured, taught what to say and how to say it, and then we got airborne in the Harvard and practised teaching each other to fly. They gave me a ride in a Prentice and to this day I am not sure if it was meant to fly or just some ones idea of a joke. Then one morning in April I was told to report to Type Flight to fly the Meteor.

I am basically a 'heavy' pilot and have an inbuilt mistrust of 'Fighter types'. My Granny once told me never to let my sister marry a fighter pilot and NEVER buy a second hand car from one. So it was with some misgivings that I trotted down to Type Flight. My instructor was Flight Sergeant (later Master Pilot) Vic Brown and on the 25th of April 1951 I was kitted up, taken around the aircraft for an exacting pre-flight inspection looking for loose rivets and skin ripples, then I was introduced to the front seat of the Meteor 7. Not a lot of room I thought to myself and indeed it was a close but comfortable fit. I followed Vic's comments around the pre-flight checks and under his control I started the engines. No noisy bangs with big things rotating, just a gentle hum and a slight vibration.....very nice I thought. As we taxied out I was impressed with the positive control of the nose wheel steering and the wonderful visibility forward. What a difference to the Harvard!

The take off was a revelation, there was the positive push from the back of the seat as we surged forward and as the speed increased so did the wind noise and the slap slap slap of the wheels as we crossed the runway expansion joints. Then the nose came up and the slap slap slap stopped and I was told to retract the wheels. There was quick thump thump thump as I moved the lever up and the wheels were all tucked up and the undercarriage warning lights were out. The airspeed indicator was winding itself up and Gloucestershire was falling behind very rapidly. I felt a part of this wonderful bird that was opening new horizons for me.

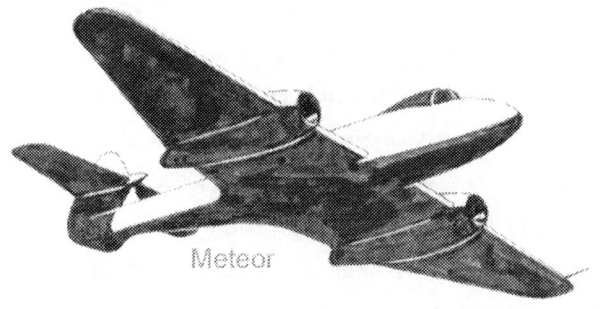

I see from my log book that the exercise was aerobatics and circuit and landings and I remember that we climbed to about twenty five grand (see I'm talking like a fighter type already, grand means thousands of feet) and I had reached there, higher and faster than ever before. We did a couple of clearing turns and went into the aerobatics exercise. I was very impressed by the ease in which it was possible to loop, roll and stall turn and I began to experience a little of what Pilot Officer Magee wrote so poetically about in 'High Flight'. We dived back towards Little Rissington when at about 4,000 feet the whole cockpit canopy misted over. I was definitely unhappy. I like to be able to look around but fortunately the front heated window was still clear but it was not very big!. The voice from the back seat told me that we had to fly around at about three hundred knots to warm the canopy up and clear the mist, we did this and things returned to normal, but I was not impressed and knocked off some 'brownie points' for this somewhat dangerous exercise.

Landings were easy compared with tail draggers and again I experienced the power of the jet and the exhilaration of the acceleration as we flew a couple of circuits and landings before we had to call it a day because the fuel state was getting low.

I was completely hooked. I did another flight with Vic Brown a week later when we investigated the asymmetric qualities of the aircraft and I realised that I needed a strong leg at times to keep control. I went back to flying the Prentice at 70 knots for a week before I was called back to Type Flight for another ride, this time with Flight Lieutenant Devillez. We climbed to 35,000 feet for an introduction to compressibility at high Mach number then a let down back to Little Rissington for a couple of circuits and landings before the fuel state made us taxi in!.

I flew as a basic instructor for three and a half years before I flew a jet again. I was lucky to be offered a three week course on the Meteor at Tarrant Rushton, the flying school being run by Flight Refuelling. My instructor was a long gangling Scot called Flying Officer Jock Miller and Jock is now the Secretary and Standard Bearer of the Ille de France Paris Branch of the Aircrew Association, small world isn't it. On the 22nd of February 1954 I flew my first single seat aircraft, a Meteor 3, I remember thinking that Granny would not be pleased!

Later that year the flying training school at Moreton in Marsh where I was stationed was scheduled to close so I applied for a jet instructors course and in October 1954 I was back at RAF Little Rissington learning the instructional patter but this time from the back seat of a Meteor. I was thirty one years old and some of my fellow students looked awfully young. They obviously knew a lot more about jet flying than me but I had three and a half thousand hours under my belt so I felt I could keep my end up.

I passed the course on 31st December 1954 and the day after I learned that I had been awarded the Air Force Medal for Instructional Duties. I continued to instruct on the Meteor 7 and the Vampire T11 for five years, enjoying every minute of it. In 1958 I was offered a weeks course on the Hunter 4 and I flew this beautiful aircraft for eight hours that week, that was the pinnacle of my jet experience. By this time I had served for twelve years in Training Command with only a three months break during 1957 at the Officers Training Unit, did I say a break, Ha!. In 1960 I was working in Changi (Singapore) Operations, every now and again, my eyes would mist over and I would be aerobating above the clouds and slow rolling without loosing a foot. Granny would have been pleased about that.

WALLY'S ASHES OR WHAT WE DID WAS ILLEGAL

by Anonymous *Best wishes Peter Crouch*

Wally was a war time Wop/AG, he was a good member of the branch and could be seen quietly enjoying a chat most club evenings. Every now and then I would ask him if he would have a beer but generally he would say that he had just taken a tablet for his heart problem so thank you, no. He came from some where North of the Watford gap and lived quietly with his wife on the edge of Boscombe.

He asked my wife if she would organise his funeral when he died but she, quite rightly said, you have a family and they should do it, so he tried another tack and asked me if I would scatter his ashes over Hurn airport. It appears that he had flown Whitleys out of Hurn during the war and was keen that his ashes should be scattered in remembrance of those days. Without giving it too much thought I said I would.

I was not sure what he wanted, did he want to be scattered to the winds from the Control Tower veranda like some one scattering wheat in the olden days, no, it appeared that he had his heart set on being scattered from an aeroplane. I liked Wally and I wondered what I had let myself in for but he was after all a friend and buddy.

In due course Wally passed away and left a letter telling us what he required us to do, it had the address of Cloud Nine on it so obviously he was on harping duties. The cremation passed off as well as these sombre events go and I started to give thoughts to Wally's final distribution. Why couldn't he have asked to be an egg timer like the rest of us? I mentioned it to a clerical friend of mine who also flies an aeroplane and he agreed to participate. To throw ashes out of an aeroplane over an airport does not hold much favour with the airport authorities and the local council and I am not too sure about the Statute of Limitation either. My clerical friend and I agreed that we would do it but did not fix a firm date.

About two months later I saw the Padre and told him that I kept hearing Wally's voice saying " What's the hold up, when are you going to do it then?" "Funny you should say that" said the Reverend " I keep hearing Wally's voice saying much the same" so we made a decision - this coming Friday. We invited two of Wally';s close friends along, arranging to meet them by the Light Aircraft Parking Area on Hurn Airport at 8:00 am. I booked a Piper Cherokee and collected Wally's ashes from the undertaker.

WALLY'S ASHES

We were sitting in the lounge watching television and Charlotte, that's my wife, said "where's Wally" "In the garage" I replied "You are not going to leave him out there all night are you?" she asked. "Oh yes I bloody am" I said and she accused me of being a cruel, heartless, uncaring beast. I'll get you for this Wally, I thought to myself.

Friday dawned bright and blue and at 8:00am the Padre and I met up with Bob and Phil at the Light Aircraft parking Area. I asked Bob to inspect the back end of the Cherokee, after all he was an ex Flight Engineer, while I did the front. Bob could not see why we were messing about with an aeroplane when we there to scatter Wally's ashes, so I told him, we are doing it from the air. They took some persuading and arm twisting but I finally got them into the back seat of the Cherokee and off we went. It was a beautiful day and it seemed a pity that Wally should be distributed without a final look around the local area so we decided to take him for a ride. Heading first to Wimborne, then Sandbanks and flying along the Bournemouth seafront at 1,000 feet we arrived at Hengistbury Head. It was now time to do what we had promised Wally we would do. We asked Hurn for an approach to runway 26 followed by a low overshoot but there was a snag, The Cherokee does not have a big side window, it has a small 'bad weather' window that faces pretty much in the direction the aircraft is heading and I realised that I might have made a mistake in hiring a Cherokee!

Too late to change things I handed control over to the Padre (who is no mean Sky Pilot) and prepared the plastic bag to be emptied. As we overshot I punctured the bag with a ball point pen and emptied the ashes out of the window. Well that was the idea but some how twenty percent of the ashes were blown back over Bob and Phil who were choking and spluttering in the back. I suddenly realised that as well as flying the aeroplane the Padre was reading the funeral service from a large prayer book and we were still going down, it looked as though that funeral service could soon apply to us. Fortunately the prayers were short ones and we were soon climbing away. After I had landed I was under the impression that we were all glad that we were back on the ground with Wally finally laid to rest.

Looking back it was hilarious and I'm sure that Wally would have chuckled as we did when it was all over, well very nearly, there were a few ashes left in the bag when I arrived home so Charlotte put them round the roses because Wally loved roses and she was convinced they would grow ten feet tall. Please have your ashes disposed of in a normal conventional way and remember that dispersing ashes from the air is not allowed.

Editors Note re-Wally's ashes by anonymous.
So far 17 members have expressed a wish that their ashes be scattered over Hurn airport. I would suggest we should leave the arrangements to 'Anonymous' as he has considerable experience and perhaps a donation £5:00 to defray costs would be appreciated.

A LOCAL DELICACY

By Peter Crouch

Many years ago when I was with the Far East Air Force I was detached for a week to Labuan Island just off Borneo. Having an interest in local customs and traditions I wandered round the local market and as is natural about mid day I wanted my lunch. I have no hang ups about eating in local food shops (as long as I have a good foundation of medicinal brandy in my tum) so I started to look for somewhere to eat.

I approached a Malay who had a food stall and asked him what he had on offer, "Poi" he said. I was very interested to know what ingredients went into this unusual native dish. "Ah, it depends" he told me "Because it comes in different forms, there is steak and kidney poi, beef and onion poi, and even apple poi"

FLYING CAN BE BORING

I was stationed at RAF Oakington flying the Varsity aircraft initiating young gentlemen into the problems of twin engine flying. On this particular day the weather was bad, why we ever got airborne I shall never know, probably the Flight Commander had a 'liver on'. We all arrived back overhead at the same time and we were stacked over the airfield at 1,000 feet intervals waiting our turn to land. Who was on top? You guessed it - me! After what seemed hours of circling I pressed the radio transmit button and said " I am bloody bored" As quick as a flash Oakington tower came back and said "Aircraft calling Oakington, say your call sign" and just as quick I replied "I'm not that bloody bored"

"T" FOR TOMMY
HOW I CAME TO LAND ON A Q SITE IN 1941

By W, F "Chappie" Chapman.

It was Jim, my second pilots` 4th trip so, as he would have his own aircraft and crew as captain next time he went over, I let him do all the flying on this trip. We took off from RAF Methwold in Wellington T for Tommy of 57 Squadron for a bombing raid somewhere over Germany. We met up with the usual flak, which Jim coped with quite well as he did with the bombing run over the target. There was more flak returning up the Ruhr. We were above cloud when we crossed the enemy coast on return, so no pin point to verify position.

Five minutes before E.T.A. English coast, as instructed we let down below cloud and fired off Very light colours of the period. It was dark with intermittent moon through broken cloud. However there was one thing missing, namely the English coast. Of course it will come up soon. As Jim was doing all the flying, he had a seat pack parachute, whereas I had a chest pack. Eventually the fuel state was looking grim, so with a possible chance of having to ditch the aircraft, as Captain I decided to take over and told the crew to get in their ditching positions. After another five minutes or so we crossed the coast and I cancelled the ditching positions for the crew. Instead I told them I would climb, and to be prepared. to bale out. Meanwhile Jim had been wandering about the fuselage with this dirty great seat pack parachute under him, and on passing the navigators position he was told he looked like a horse and cart, in as much as, back at the main spar, his parachute had become trapped, thereby, when he came forward again, his harness was extended. He turned to go back for his back- pack, don't ask me how he did it, but he finished up with his arms full of parachute silk and shrouds.

Meanwhile I'm busy in the cockpit, we had reached 7000 feet and about to tell everyone to get out, when I got this tap on the shoulder from Jim who was standing behind me with his arms full of silk. "Don't make me jump skipper" he said, I'll break me ruddy neck".

I had a problem, with not much time to sort it out as the fuel gauges had been on empty for some time, and the engines might stop at any time. I asked my navigator Ron, if we had an operational flare that we could drop to light up the ground in order for me to find a suitable field in which to land. He had one and dropped it, and the sky lit up. The crew had heard all this going on over the R/T and decided they would rather take their chance by staying with the aircraft in the hope that I would pull off, which after all was a very dicey performance. I'm still at 7000 feet and not very comfortable as I had no neat pack to sit on. In and out of cloud I began to let down when to my joy, up ahead off the port bow was a flare- path.

Being on a long base leg I continued to let down and at 800 feet turned onto final approach, now I'm lined up with the flare-path. It looked like a donkey's hind leg. Then all hell broke loose, red Very lights were coming up thick and fast. I'd already got the crew into crash positions and told them to be prepared for a rough landing. No way could I risk going round again with an overshoot, not knowing when the fuel would finally run out and the fans stop. Just as I was stalling off for a touch- down an enormous gaping hole appeared beneath me, so I hit full throttles and she responded. Having left the hole behind I sat the kite down, talk about up hill and down dale.

We were down, the nose turret was just inside the branches of a small wood. I switched off, opened the window to see three chaps with rifles milling about the aircraft. I called out "Is this England" and got the reply "Yus mate" We got out and inspected the Wellington, the only damage was the trailing aerial weights had been snapped off. We went down into the decoy crews deep shelter. The Q site on which we landed was manned by a Corporal and three airmen. The Cpl. was intrigued as to how I had missed "his" hole, which had camouflage netting stretched over. My landing lights were the saving grace there, in as much they had shone through the netting and presented the hole to me, how friendly can you get?. The ground was as soft as pudding, hence the smoothness sensation despite the undulations!! At dawn the Cpl. took me to see the said hole and camouflage netting. Using the decoy sites telephone I rang my C.O. at RAF Methwold who wanted to know the damage to the aircraft. He was pleased when I said the only damage was the weights on the aerial, then he said there's an air raid in progress, once it's over I'll send transport over to collect you. Then he started to laugh and said "you're the air raid", It would appear my flare had put the best part of Norfolk into air raid shelters. As its a Courts Marshal offence to drop operational flares over your own territory, I was in a state of flux for a few days, until the powers that be decided that the action I had taken was correct under the circumstances prevailing. The decoy site was KQ.28 at

Snarehill, near Thetford, Norfolk. The incident was recorded as such. Early one morning, a bomber returning from a raid, landed on the flare-path, how the pilot managed to get down we shall never know as the ground was a rabbit warren that caved in as you walked on it. Mr. F. Feltham was in charge of Snarehill decoy site.

PRINCE EUGEN-BISMARK

W F Chapman

As a Sergeant Pilot in the R.A.F.V.R (No.754772) I was called up on the 1st Sept.1939, as war was declared on the 3rd of September

The following is an account of an unsuccessful effort to get the Prince Eugen which had been keeping company with the Bismark. At the time, I was still a Sgt Pilot of a Wellington 1c, belonging to 57 Squadron, 3 Group, Bomber Command, stationed at Feltwell, Norfolk.

One afternoon, the powers that be decided that the squadron should practice formation flying. This we had never done before, as night bombers went over on their own, needless to say, I suppose when it was a full moon, there was no real reason why we couldn't have gone over in formation, but in the early days of the war, it wasn't general practice so to do. However this particular afternoon we were flying one hours practice at formation. You can imagine the comments among the crews why we had been ordered to do this, and we soon found out.

We were called to the briefing room, where we were informed that the 'Bismark' had been located, and briefed as to how we were going to attack it. The Squadron Leader of 'A' Flight and myself (the senior pilots on the squadron) were to carry 'B' type mines, and drop them as a 'stick' from 1,000 feet. I was to drop mine across its starboard bow, and the Squadron Leader dropping his across its port bow, so that no matter which way it turned, BINGO! nice game, I don't think. With the fire power the Bismark had on it, our chances of survival were nil. The remainder of the squadron had armour piercing bombs. From this point on, we were confined to camp, for obvious reasons. There was no way I could get a message to my wife, and I hoped she would see us taking off at dawn, otherwise, if she just heard the general noise of aircraft at dawn, she might think it was the noise of aircraft returning from a raid, and that I had failed to return. We all hung around in our rooms, myself in with my second pilot, where there was a spare bed to relax on.

In the small hours of the morning the tannoy went, ordering all aircrew to report to the briefing room. We were informed that the Bismark had been hit by a torpedo, and was in a crippled state, and the navy was engaging to finish it off. Our plan of attack remained the same, but now we would be going after the 'Prince Eugen', which had been keeping company with the Bismark. We were given a suspected position about 60 miles off Brest, where we could hope to engage it.

Came dawn, visibility very poor, cloud base 500ft. The Squadron Leader and myself would be in the same flight, both carrying our load of 'A' type mines. There were four Wellingtons in this flight, and the Squadron Leader decided we would take off in formation, which we did. Unfortunately, he led us right into the cloud, and we had no option but to break formation and hope to re-group above the cloud. This didn't work out in practice, but I wasn't too worried, as we had decided we would re-group over Lands End, should we get split up. Seeing that we had taken off from Feltwell in Norfolk, it took some little time to get to Lands End, which we eventually did, where I let down below cloud (base about 1,200ft, visibility 2 to 3 miles). We had been told that on no account should we go out on our own, due to the fact that we were in black bombers, and the firepower in formation is far better than that of a single aircraft.

We didn't have long to wait before three Wellingtons arrived in formation. I closed with them, but they weren't my three!!. This happened two or three times with the same result, time was getting on. The next three Wellingtons to come along were from the other squadron at my airfield, so I called up the leader on R/T told him the position, and asked if I could fly box position with him. This he agreed, and off we went. Flying box formation as number four which is slightly behind and a little below the V formation. Eventually we arrive at the position where we hoped the Prince Eugene should have been. There were aircraft all over the place, but no battleship!!. My Navigator had religiously kept his log going. The formation had a short discussion about which direction we should proceed, in order to intercept our target, and it was decided we would try a little further North. The cloud base was varying between 1,000 and 1,200ft, with visibility between 2 to 4 miles. We hadn't been going more than 15 minutes on our new heading, when two dots appeared off our starboard bow, flying just below the cloud base. They were too far away to determine what they were, but I was mighty suspicious of them, even more so when they pulled up into the cloud at a point off our starboard beam. I told the crew to keep their eyes peeled and to watch out for a possible attack from the rear quarter, or dead astern!! When fighters attack bombers in formation, they usually go for number 4 at the back. The aircraft I was flying was a new one. It was its first operational trip.

I had positioned my second pilot in the astrodome, just in case we were going to experience an attack from the rear, in which case he could give me pertinent information of the attack so that I could act accordingly. We hadn't long to wait before the dreaded report of "Enemy fighters attacking from the starboard quarter!". Rocky Red Leader (the call sign of the leading aircraft of the formation) gave instructions to go; "Down on the deck", for it was sea in whichever direction one looked, but we all knew what he meant. Mind you, a fully laden Wellington is no match for fighter aircraft in broad daylight. These two were Arado float planes, of the type carried by the Prince Eugene. I knew I would have my work cut out to stay up with the rest of the formation, due to my aircraft being new, and a bit stiff, performance wise. Do I go down, or should I just ease back the column, and take full cover just above me. I decided to go down with them, in the hope that I could keep up in formation, where our combined fire power would do the trick.

It didn't take long before we were all down to 50ft, going flat out. I was the only aircraft under attack, being at the rear of the formation, so I was the only one having to weave from side to side, with the surface of the sea being turned into Persil, first under the port wing, then under the starboard wing. However, this erratic course I had to steer resulted in me becoming a 'straggler' and falling behind the formation by more than somewhat!!.

My second pilot let out a yell. He had been hit as a bullet passed across the back of his hand, scorching a groove-no blood!!. In his words, some engine covers on the bed (adjacent to his legs as he stood at the astrodome) suddenly got up, did a dance and fell down in ribbons! My rear gunner reported a stoppage in one of his Browning's, at the same time advising me that the starboard elevator had been shot away, and the top third of the rudder had gone.

By now, the three aircraft up ahead of me were some 150yds away and Rocky Red Leader gave orders for us to jettison our bombs. I thought this a bit rich, as I was the one being fired at not them. However, orders are orders, so I also jettisoned my mines. It would appear in hindsight that I was just in time, as I received a direct hit in the bomb bay, resulting in three of the bomb bay doors hanging off, and a floatation bag inflating and hanging out of the bottom of the aircraft. Along with this, the hydraulics system went, resulting in one undercarriage leg falling down, whilst the other remained up. By now I was anything but streamlined, and really falling way back.

The number two aircraft of the formation ahead (call sign Harry) was calling Rocky Red unrepeatable names, and demanding that they all fall back to assist Yours Truly, who anyone could see was in a bit of trouble, to put it mildly. However, not a peep came back from the leader, so H Harry told me to hang on as he would fall back. This he did by dropping his undercarriage and flaps, thus reducing speed by more than somewhat, and tucked in beside me. The sudden manoeuvre caught the fighters off guard, and the rear gunners managed to score a hit on one of them. It is not known whether he brought it down or not. Then, as quick as the action started, it was over. Eventually, we regrouped the formation, and proceeded in the direction of Lands End.

During the engagement, my transmitter had been damaged, so I couldn't talk to the rest of the formation on the R/T, but I could still receive!. First of all, they had great concerns about the state of my aircraft, and were heard to say that they didn't envy my job of keeping the thing airborne, and that the formation would make for St.Eval for my benefit. This did not fit in with my plans at all, due to the fact that my dear wife had most likely spent the whole of that day grieving for a lost husband. I told my navigator that on reaching St.Eval, my intention was to proceed to base, if he could route me adjacent to airfields en route, providing that by so doing, we would reach base with a margin of fuel left. He estimated that we had lost some 30 gallons of fuel during the fight, and had worked out a route which should get us home with some 20 minutes of spare fuel. Of course, due to lack of a transmitter, on reaching St.Eval, I was unable to appraise the other three aircraft of my intentions, so they went in and landed, but I set course for home!!. The aircraft behaved quite well, considering the shape it was in, and we duly arrived over base, though I could not talk to them. However, after a few low passes, they soon got the messages that some thing wasn't quite right, as for a start, it was unusual for Wellingtons to fly around with one wheel up and one wheel down, so they sort of got ready for the worst!; Our main concern was to get both wheels down and locked, to which end we all took turns to pump them into the locked position with the emergency hand pumps-no joy! We were all, exhausted, with nothing to show for it. I did not want to sit her down with one undercart just hanging down, unlocked. We tried to pump it up, out of the way - no joy. By now, the fuel state is not good. I had decided I would have to land it on one wheel!. Then an idea came to me. I asked the crew if they had any coffee left in their Thermos flasks. They all had. I asked the Radio Operator if he could detach the pipe that led to the emergency hydraulic tank (above his head). He did, and all the thick, gooey dregs from our Thermos flasks were tipped in. Result - undercarriage down and locked on coffee!. I still couldn't work the flaps, but managed a flapless landing without further damage to the aircraft. We touched down at 110 m.p.h. and stopped at the edge of the field after missing a few obstacles on the way.

Extent of damage. Three doors hanging off the bomb bay and seven feet missing from starboard wing. The starboard elevator shot away and the top third of rudder missing, The hydraulic system was damaged and there were twelve holes in fuel tank (self sealing, thank God), we also had a variety of holes in both wings and central fuselage. Plus, as I had correctly thought, a very worried wife who thought I was missing.

NEEDLE AND BALL

By Jim Bevis

Early in my flying training in the Autumn of 1944 at No.3 British Flying Training School, Miami, Olkahoma, I took off with my American civilian primary flying instructor, Mr.Vic Tidswell (see accompanying photograph) for a session of instrument flying. This involved pulling a folding canvas hood over, thus depriving one of all references to the outside world.

F/ins. Vic Tidswell

The PT19, a monoplane that we flew, had open cockpits unlike the Canadian version, the Cornell which had a cockpit canopy for the colder winters. We also had a metal crash pylon between the two cockpits to protect us, we hoped, in the case of a prang.

Having pulled the hood over as ordered and surveyed the instrument panel, I saw that the needle and ball indicator, the most revered blind flying instrument of American instructors, was not working I reported this and was told to push back the hood and that I had control and to fly straight and level. Suddenly I saw him standing up, turning and holding on to the pylon like grim death, putting one leg over the side and then the other, and working his way back on the wing so that he could see the offending instrument. Needless to say, he kept his parachute on for this performance. Sticking his head in the cockpit he shouted at me to kick the rudder and seeing, much to my relief that there was no response, made his way to his cockpit and so, we went home.

Nothing more was said, and apart from the occasional flick roll (strictly forbidden), sometimes at night, the primary course came to an end. Having told my fellow course students of this, one thought he may have done this before and so perhaps he was just keeping his hand in for one of his pre-war jobs in a barn storming outfit.

Editors Note :- I'm surprised that the instructor did not suggest that Jim should climb over and change places with him as the needle and ball instrument in the front seat was working ok.

MOON OVER NORWAY

By Fl Lt Stan Sickelmore

My memories of operating with 138 Special Duty Squadron from Tempsford are of an unusually quiet airfield. Not because it wasn't a busy place, but it was a very secret place, and we had few visits from high ranking officers or politicians. We were not permitted to talk freely about any aspect of our work to anybody. The local people knew nothing of what we did. Another reason was that our aircraft, Short Stirling MkIV`s were fitted with Bristol Hercules XVII air-cooled sleeve valve radial engines and were remarkably quiet. A distinct advantage when flying low over enemy territory, and thirdly we operated individually to different targets at varying times, so there was rarely a great gaggle of planes starting up and taking off at the same time.

On the night of 30th.September 1944 we were destined to take a load of supplies to the Norwegian resistance, to a drop near Honefoss north east of the Telemark area. We slipped quietly into the sky at 2144 hrs and crossed the North Sea at 1500 feet, until we were approaching the Skagerrak with the coast of Jutland a way to our right. At this point I descended to about 150 feet. As we approached Kristiansand I climbed over the coast keeping just above the mountain-tops. Everything was covered in snow which was quite blinding in the dull moonlight. My bomb-aimer mapped us to the target and the resistance group flashed the code, two whites and a red and the correct letter. So we completed the drop of twelve containers from the bomb bay and twelve large packages from the fuselage hatch. The latter were pushed out by the dispatcher, who would have been our Mid-upper gunner if we'd had a turret for him. I should perhaps mention at this point that the MkIV .had been stripped of its mid upper turret, and the front turret had been replaced with a smooth Perspex dome which afforded the bomb-aimer much better vision all round, for low level map reading. The aircraft was also made lighter, more streamlined and a bit faster.

We turned for home at about 0230 hrs and were just approaching the Norwegian coast when our rear gunner said that a Messerschmitt 110 was approaching fast from astern. I can't remember our altitude, but we had been flying just above the tops of the mountains, so we were probably about 4000 feet. I pushed the nose down and opened the throttles fully, the idea being to get as low over the sea as possible, as fast as possible. I pulled out of the dive and levelled out at between 100 and 50 feet keeping the speed at maximum. We lost the fighter so I eased off the power and continued over the water at 100 feet. During the dive we achieved an airspeed of 375 mph. which was 65 mph over the recommended limit for the aircraft. All four engines had over heated but were now under control and within limits. We were safe, or so we thought. A few minutes later we were in the middle of a stream of light anti aircraft fire, which was coming from a flak ship that we had failed to see. They were often positioned off the Danish coast, and moved around so it was impossible to forecast their positions. Due to our low altitude and still fairly high speed, the arc of fire from the ship was short and we were clear within seconds. We suffered no hits.

We continued back to Tempsford, landing at 0650 hrs after a flight of nine hours and four minutes. We de-briefed, had some breakfast, and went to bed. We later found that we were not over popular with the engineers, who had to change all four of the engines after my rough treatment. Still, at least they had the aircraft to work on and a crew who survived to fly it again.

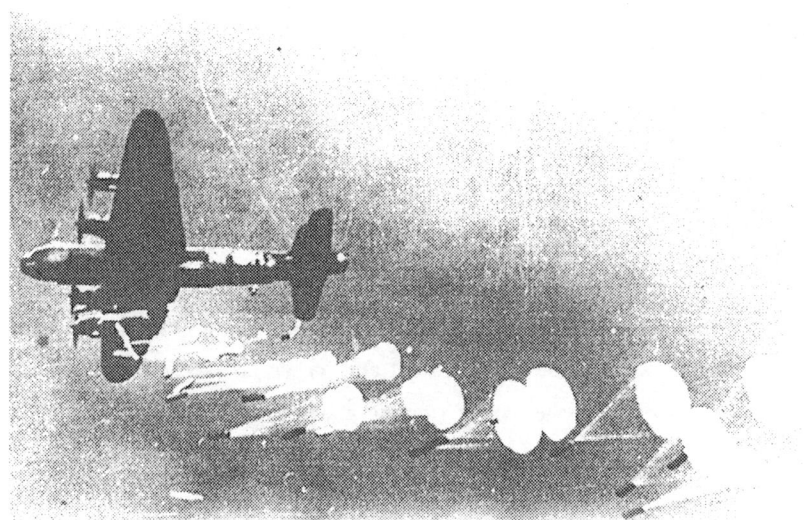

138 Sqdn Dropping supplies to Belgium White Army 1944

ABOVE THE BATTLE OF THE BULGE

By Stan Sickelmore

It was Xmas Eve 1944, and all of us on 138 Special Duty Squadron hoped that we would not be required for operations that night. But alas our hopes were dashed when we were called for briefing quite early in the day. We were used to doing many different tasks. Dropping supplies and agents to various resistance groups throughout occupied Europe and Scandinavia. Carrying out diversion raids for main force, daylight drops to the Belgian resistance just ahead of the Allied invasion forces, and now to take a small part in the Battle of the Bulge.

Our load this time was not containers of supplies, but dummy parachutists loaded with fire crackers and explosive devices, also dropped by parachute that would explode on, or nearing the ground. These were to be dropped behind enemy lines and deceive them into thinking that an airborne force would be attacking them from their rear. It was hoped that they would divert some troops in that direction thus weakening the front at that point, as the Allies made a determined attack. Whether it worked at all I don't know, but since the battle went on for so long after that, it's doubtful. Maybe General Von Rundstedt saw through our little ploy.

We took off at 1610z and flew at 1500 feet. Our task was to make the drop from 1000 feet near the town of Prum. It was a very dark night but with very good visibility. I descended to 1000 feet and as we crossed over the battle area we could see the flashes of the opposing artillery fire brilliantly against the dark ground and artillery flares lighting up different areas. All hell seemed to have broken loose down there. It was an awesome sight, and the picture remains vividly in my memory to this day. We completed the drop successfully, our fire-crackers made a fine display, and we turned for home. We crossed the lines but saw little this time as we were climbing to return at a higher altitude.

Tempsford and most of the south of England was closed in with fog, so we were diverted to Lyneham, where conditions were a little better. We landed at 2145z, and were in time to join in their Xmas party. However, the weather clamped down for two days so we were unable to fly back to base until the day after Boxing day. All that time wearing our flying gear, and only borrowed toiletries!. Still, we had New Years Eve to look forward to. No, on the 31st we were on our way to supply the Danish resistance. But that's another story.

Many years later, I met a chap who told me that he was at the Battle of the Bulge fighting on the ground in the mud and filth. I told him of what I had seen, that I and my crew had all said" God I'm glad we are not down there". He laughed, that's what I used to say when I saw your planes flying over, "I'm glad I'm not up there". I bought him a pint, I thought it was the least I could do.

FATAL ENCOUNTER

By Stan McCreith.

In 1942/43 I was on loan to the U.S. Army Air Corps as a flying instructor on Harvards doing advanced training of American students at Napier Field, Dotham, Alabama. This was their final training for their wings and commissions. We concentrated on the normal exercises of formation, navigation, gunnery, aerobatics, instrument flying and elementary combat. One exercise required the student to follow the lead regardless. The chase

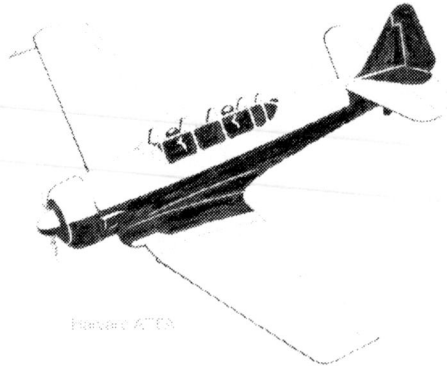

aircraft had to maintain position at all times. Mid January '43 I took off on a similar exercise with my student, 2nd Lt. Pedigo (who had been commissioned a few days before) in one Harvard chasing and a further student as my passenger in another for the experience. After a series of manoeuvres I built up speed and pulled up into a loop. I could see Pedigo following. As I reached the top of the loop the Harvard suddenly flicked over into a violent spin. I applied the normal recovery with no response and all the controls were completely slack. I assumed structural failure and decided to find another way home. I instructed my student to bail out and slid back the canopy, counting to four before pulling the rip cord. At this point I regretted that I had not been in the habit of pulling my parachute tight, particularly the leg straps, while my voice did not go up an octave or two, I suffered some discomfort in the nether regions for the next day or two. Hanging in the chute I saw another parachute some two thousand feet above me so I knew the student with me was safe. To my surprise my aircraft had come out of the spin and entered a spiral around me. As it passed in front of me, some few hundred feet away, I was amazed to see the whole tailplane, fin and rudder, was missing, structural failure it certainly was. There were pieces of aluminium and other debris in the air, together with my map from my overall pocket. From my vantage point I watched the Harvard crash into a field and shed its wings and I landed in the next field, collapsed the chute, bundled it up and walked to the wreck. I spoke to two farm workers who told me that there was another crashed aircraft on the other side of the road with a "dead fella in it". I had lost one student and the lost tailplane was explained. Pedigo must have lost sight of me and chopped my tail off, no doubt being killed or knocked out in the collision. His plane was a total wreck and would have fitted into an average sitting room. I lost a pair of Ray Ban sunglasses.

P R U
680 MOSQUITO SQUADRON

By Stan McCreith.

1944 saw me in the Middle East, in 680 Photographic Reconnaissance Squadron with its headquarters at Kilo 8 (Payne Field to the Americans), with a detached flight of Spitfire 11's in Cyprus and a flight of Mosquito P.R.16's at Tocra in North Africa not far from Benghazi. The Mosquito flight was moved to San Severo in Italy from where we could cover most of Europe, out to the Russian Front and overlapping the cover of the Benson Squadrons. Some operations became decidedly dicey. Although the Mosquito 16 was very fast and could reach high altitudes, the Germans now had the Messerschmitt 262 jets in service, which meant it could overtake on the climb out of sight under your tail. The first warning would be cannon shells floating past!. We normally operated at 30,000ft out of the range of the 88mm guns as the 105mm were mostly used in heavily defended areas. The Mosquito's were fitted with two F52-36 inch cameras and a 6" survey camera for plotting purposes. Successive exposures controlled by a type 35 control had a 60% overlap to produce stereo pairs of photographs.

Wellingtons were used to lay mines in the enemy rivers and in October 44 my navigator, Don Pizzey, and I had the job of photographing the Danube from Vienna to Budapest, looking for sunken shipping. We arrived over Vienna and there was a lot of activity, the Americans were bombing a refinery on the outskirts of the city, we had to come down to 28,000 ft. to clear some cirrus, not a good move as we were chased by 88mm flak while we flew back and forth to cover the bends of the rivers. With the job finished at Budapest we headed for San Severo. Shortly afterwards all the glycol departed from the starboard engine (flack damage?) and the engine was feathered. No problem, we could get back on one engine even though we lost height. Near Lake Balaton, Hungary more accurate 88mm flak came up when over open country, surprisingly resulting in the loss of oil from the port engine. I thought foolishly, that we could flog this stricken Mosquito to Yugoslavia and hope to meet some of Tito's boys. Of course, with hindsight we should have bailed out, but the PR Mossie was awkward to get out of and the crew could not stay together. We altered course for the nearest point Yugoslavia and pressed on putting faith in the Rolls Royce engines. We went a surprisingly long way until the vibrations from the port engine told me the bearings were going, so I unfeathered the starboard and feathered the port. This engine also took us a fair way but not to Tito land and we crash landed off the south end of Lake Balaton.

Everything went wrong, I overshot the selected field because the flaps did not go down (only one windmilling engine) and I could not get rid of the speed. As a result we carved through a wood, making our own runway and slid out at the far side on fire and sitting like the Wright brothers with nothing in front. I was unconscious among other things and Don had a broken arm. Somehow he dragged me out of the wreckage, I cannot guess how, otherwise I would have been a cremation job. So I owe him a lifetime debt. One other thing I should mention, it was Friday 13th October, I lost another pair of Ray Ban sunglasses and was relieved of an expensive watch. I had been heavily concussed and my memories are therefore sketchy, particularly in time. We were in hospital for a while and quite well treated as far as I can remember, and then put on a train with a couple of armed guards to Budapest and into solitary confinement in, I believe, a civil gaol which may have been a collection point for downed Allied aircrew. One night I stood on the end of my bed to look out of a small high window to watch an air raid by the Russians on Budapest. Twin engined aircraft zooming about at low level in what appeared to be a random fashion unloading small bombs here and there.

After a time a number of R.A.F and U.S. aircrew were taken down to Budapest and loaded into a cattle truck to be given a ride across Europe finishing at Dulag Luft near Frankfurt on Maine, the German interrogation centre for Allied aircrew. It was now some weeks since I was shot down so my interrogation was fairly perfunctory. Also by this time it must have been obvious to the Germans that they had lost the war. I was questioned by a Luftwaffe major who spent nearly all his time talking to me about his

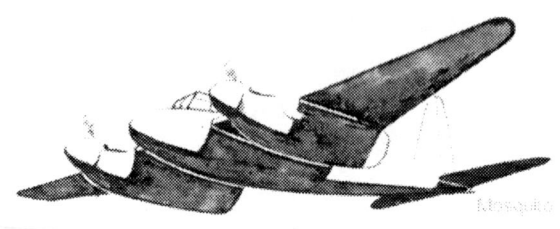

experiences as a POW in W.W.1. He did ask me two or three times about H2S but I had not the foggiest idea what he was talking about. Another train journey, this time in proper carriages and I arrived at Stalag Luft 3, a more than somewhat bedraggled RAF Flt Lt. who now had further interrogation by the senior officers in the camp to establish my true identity. Incidentally I had lost my dog tags somewhere along the line although this was never a critical factor. I had been parted from Don at Dulag Luft because he was a Warrant Officer and went to a different camp. Satisfied with my identity I was allotted to a hut where the senior officer was Wg. Cdr. R.R. Stamford-Tuck with a bunch of cheerful coves who made me most welcome. By now it was just before Christmas 44 and the food situation was not too bad with supplies of Red Cross parcels. Also Stalag Luft 3 was an old and well established prison camp near Breslau in Upper Silesia, however the winters were very cold in Eastern Europe so the temperatures were sub zero nearly all the time.

In January 45 the Russians were advancing steadily and we could hear the gunfire in the East and started to hope that release by the Russians might be fairly soon. No such luck, the Germans came in one night and we were ordered out at gunpoint to trek to the west. We stalled all night but then had to set off in a long straggling column with guards at intervals on each side. I think this march has been well documented elsewhere, suffice it to say that our lot finished up south of Berlin, at Luckenwalde Concentration Camp. Conditions were not good and the food situation was minimal, with no Red Cross food parcels coming through. The Allied air offensive with massive interdiction was making it very difficult for the Germans to move anything, so the country was grinding to a halt. Finally the Russians arrived, with mortar shells going over the camp and the Germans in retreat, a Russian tank column arrived and mowed down some of the barbed wire fences. They were unsmiling and in no way friendly, I thought then they would only pause until the defeat of Germany and then be on the move again for the rest of Western Europe. I was right but it was a cold war and a not a hot W.W.111 that developed.

On one occasion we had a grand stand view of Bomber Command attacking Potsdam and it was a most impressive sight with the sky markers going down and the flashes of exploding ordnance. The Germans certainly reaped the whirlwind, deservedly in my opinion.

One day a column of U.S. Army trucks arrived to take us back for repatriation and we all filed aboard with our meagre possessions. This was not to be, the Russians turned out and we were ordered off the trucks at gunpoint and the U.S. Army trucks drove away empty. Shattering to say the least and we wondered if we were destined for Siberia, such was our faith in the Russians. However, they explained it was their responsibility to arrange repatriation but first they wanted to make sure no German war criminals were hiding in the camp. So we were all processed through a registration procedure, they would not accept our assurances that no German could slip through our own vetting system. There was a hotchpotch of the nations of Europe at Luchenwalde and I have no idea of what happened to many of them. No doubt many would have finished up in Siberia. Came the day when a column of Russians trucks arrived and we were driven to the river crossing where we were handed over to the Americans.

After some leave and a Buckingham Palace garden party I could not wait to get airborne again, so off I went for another stint at Benson at the Photographic Reconnaissance Development Unit which gave me a taste for test flying.

AN ACT OF GOD

By Slim Pocock

Entry in a Bomber Command Accident Report.
Aircraft. Avro Lincoln. WD148. No.100 Squadron Royal Air Force Wittering. 27th August 1953 at 22:41 hrs. Pilot F.Sgt .W. Ryba Total solo flying hours 4224, hours on type 341.

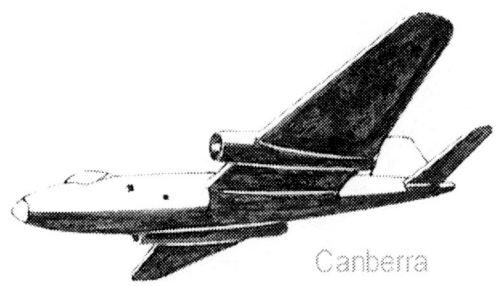

At 18,000 feet and approximately 30 seconds after releasing a bomb on a practice Gee-H-detail a violent explosion took place in the rear of the aircraft. On checking it was found that none of the crew was injured and the aircraft was still responding normally to the flying controls. The aircraft returned to base without further incident. After landing it was found that the aircraft had been struck by a twenty five pound practice bomb from another aircraft.

Slim was a navigator and was helping to 'screen' a crew of a Lincoln on a bombing exercise. When they landed the rudder controls fell apart, there was no Board of Inquiry as the CO said the chances of this happening were a million to one against, and that it was 'An Act of God'

Remarks: It was subsequently discovered that the bomb came from a Canberra bombing from 29,000 feet. It was confirmed that the bombing range were complying with all the bombing safety regulations, and that no evidence exists of negligence or equipment failure on the part of the crews or the aircraft bombing at the time. The chances against this type of accident recurring must be astronomical. Unavoidable Major Flying Accident

ON `YER´ BIKE ADOLF

G Serrels 166 Squadron

A large four engined bomber requires a Ground crew of men and women to keep it in an airworthy condition. Engine Fitters, Airframe Fitters, Instrument Mechanics, Radio and Radar Mechanics, Armourers, Bowser Drivers and Tractor Drivers (usually WAAF's) to tow the bomb trolleys. They take a great pride in maintaining 'Their' aircraft, working long hours to make sure it's ready for the Aircrew who will fly it on operations.

Aircrew become attached to `Their´ aircraft in the same way, and, unless it was too badly damaged, will fly it on every operation. It was not surprising then, that a bond of respect developed between Ground crew and Aircrew, which the following incident will illustrate.

The target for the night's raid was Nurenburgh, and the WAAF driving the crew bus had dropped us off at the dispersal where our Lancaster bomber and

Ground crew were waiting for us. We completed the usual pre boarding inspections of our aircraft and the Flt. Eng., Bill Swaffield, reported to me that all was OK. Then he said "We have a problem", I noted the 'we' and waited for him to continue. Bill then related the following. Nobby Clark, our Engine fitter, was in trouble. Nobby had been celebrating in the  local village the night before and had missed the last transport back to the station. To report to the guard room after 23 59 hours would have involved him in a spell of 'special duties', so he 'borrowed' a bicycle that had been left unattended (meaning to return it at the first available opportunity) and cycled

From an original painting by Keith Woodcock, GAvA

back to the station, arriving just in time to beat the midnight deadline.
So far, so good, but the owner of the bike had reported the theft to the local police, and the local police had a good idea where the bike might be, so the Service Police at the station were asked to investigate and were prowling around at this very moment. For the bike to be discovered on the station was not only bad for Nobby Clark, it would also sour relations between the squadron and the local villagers.

Bill Swaffield took a deep breath and, looking in the direction of our aircraft, said "I've put the bike in the bomb bay and checked that the doors close OK. We can drop it over Germany on the way to the target" Knowing my Flt. Eng., I was not surprised at the action he had taken, in fact I thought it a good way to solve the problem. But of course RAF discipline had to be maintained, so I replied "I haven't a clue what you are talking about" or words to that effect. Bill then went off to have a word with Nobby Clark to let him know that he was off the hook.

The exact location of the drop was not recorded, but if it survived its fall from 20,000 ft, it would make a valuable museum piece.

Since this story appeared in our first edition, several readers have complained that this action was a little irresponsible as the bike could have fallen on someone and hurt them. Editor.

WHICH WAY?

By G A Serrels 166 Squadron

When the Pilot and Navigator argue over the correct course to steer for home the rest of the crew listen in on the intercom with more than usual interest. The incident happened when the crew of Lancaster 'O' Oboe were returning from a bombing raid on a target deep inside Germany. The Ack-Ack Gunners had put up a very intensive Box Barrage which the attacking bombers were forced to fly through to reach the target. Many near misses were felt and heard as the flack rattled along the fuselage during the run in to the target.

It was the Bomb Aimer's long awaited 'Bombs Gone' that broke the tension felt by all the crew, followed by the Navigator's voice saying, "Skipper, your course for home is 292". The Skipper set the course on his gyro compass and after warning his crew to keep a sharp lookout for other aircraft, turned onto his new course.

It was several minutes later before the Navigator's voice was heard requesting the Skipper to confirm his course, with a suggestion that he might be flying a reciprocal. It was not unknown for a pilot, in the heat of the moment, to make this mistake. The Skipper checked his compass and confirmed that he was heading in a Westerly direction, but the Navigator was not convinced and said, "If you carry on in this direction we shall end up in Russia".

The rest of the crew, listening on the intercom, suddenly became more than usually attentive, not wishing to spend the rest of the war in Russia they waited anxiously for the outcome of the argument. The answer came in the form of the old fashioned magnetic compass P7, situated down by the pilot's right leg. After removing the dust from the compass and with the aid of a torch it was a relieved crew who heard the Flight Engineer confirm that the aircraft was heading in a Westerly direction.

"Oboe" returned safely to base and it was the next day when the ground crew inspected the aircraft for damage that the Instrument Mechanic suggested a possible solution to the mystery. The H2S scanner had a large hole in the front of the cupola which probably caused the scanner to rotate in the opposite direction to its norm, giving the Navigator a false indication.

G Serrels Left Front Row

THE SHEER THRILL OF BEING A MEMBER OF AN OPERATIONAL MARKING TEAM

By W. W. "BILL" Burke

IN NO WAY did I want to join 627 Squadron. I ended my first tour of operations with 207 Squadron as a non-commissioned navigator on Lancaster Main Force bombers of 5 Group, operating out of Spilsby in Lincolnshire. To be precise, my last operation was an attack in the early hours of 4 January 1945 on the Germans holding out in Royan, which was, incidentally, marked by 627. As I remember it, the beleaguered garrison had irritated the local populace by venturing out to rustle cattle. If that was so, then a visit by 5 Group's 200-250 bombers was a heavy price to pay for their fillet steak!

At the time I was twenty years of age and had been flying on operations continually since August 1944. It had been an exciting tour, full of experiences which I can still recall with astonishing clarity. For example, until I die, there will be imprinted on my mind the memory of attacking Bremen on the night of 6 October 1944. We were 'coned' by searchlights and hit by anti-aircraft fire which, amongst other things, cut the oil pipelines to the rear turret rendering the turret virtually inoperable. Then - almost immediately - the rear and mid-upper gunners began screaming that a JU88 night fighter was commencing a stern attack. We were all but defenceless and I sat there waiting for a hail of machine gun and cannon fire to come streaming down the fuselage putting paid to my life. But no - the fates were kind. Suddenly we flew into dense cloud and were lost to the night fighter.

As a consequence of such experiences I was a shade 'flak happy" In other words the strains and stresses of going into battle some 30 times and seeing so many comrades in the Squadron fail to return from raids had affected my nerves. For example, my hands had a typical 'Bomber Command Twitch which sometimes called for an effort to light a cigarette. In these circumstances you might well think that I would have been more than happy at the prospect of a safe posting possibly to an instructor's job in Training Command. But far from it - I liked the life on an operational squadron and wanted to stay there.

This may seem surprising, but my 21st birthday was still five months away and at that age one can crave excitement - danger, like drugs can become habit forming and one wants a regular 'injection' of danger and the enormous elation which one experiences when the danger is past and one is still unharmed. It was also a glamorous life. The contract was that you flew the RAF's aeroplanes with the statistical likelihood that you would be killed, wounded or taken prisoner. In return the RAF paid you well, gave you a great deal of freedom and time off, with leave every six weeks and extended to you a variety of privileges which few enjoyed in war-time Britain. These included such things as air crew meals of bacon and eggs, special sweet rations, petrol for use in private cars and sheets to sleep in. If you weren't required for flying you could do more or less what you liked; large numbers of air crew in "Bomber Counties" such as Lincolnshire largely spent their spare time in pubs and dance halls, getting "stoned" and chasing the ladies. Cities such as Nottingham were an air crew paradise and the "White Hart in Lincoln was like a 5 Group Headquarters. To turn one's back on this sort of Boys Own Paper life and the conscious pride that goes with being a member of an acknowledged corps Elite was unthinkable to me at the time. So I decided to volunteer for an immediate second tour of operations.

Looking back with the benefit of a life time's maturity it was an utterly foolish and foolhardy decision, akin to applying for and then signing one's own death warrant - but one doesn't think that way at twenty. One then has a supreme confidence and a belief that it will be the other guy who doesn't come through safely. However, I did decide that although I wanted to continue fighting, I 'wanted out' of Bomber Command. Instead I decided that I would like to fly in Beaufighters in Scotland on anti-shipping strikes. I thought that would be exciting and also that it would be satisfying in the sense that one would know whether or not one had been successful. Either a boat was there or it was sunk. Unfortunately my application for a switch to Beaufighters was turned down out of hand. I say "unfortunately" but, in fact, it might be more appropriate to use the word "Fortunately" as I later discovered that there was a very high 'chop rate' amongst air crew attacking enemy shipping guarded by flak ships.

At the same time as my transfer application was rejected I was told that if I did want to continue operational flying I could be fixed up with a navigator's job on 627 Squadron of Path Finder Force, based at Woodhall Spa. If I accepted the offer I could have a commission and so a deal was done.

Having accepted the switch somewhat reluctantly and unenthusiastically my initial impressions, when I arrived at Woodhall Spa, were not especially favourable. At Spilsbury with two squadrons of Lancaster's, each with seven to the crew, there was a very consider-able number of air crew personnel to chum up with, whereas at Woodhall there was a single squadron (617 messed quite separately from 627 Squadron) with only two crew per aircraft. So the total number of air crew with whom to make friends and associate was quite small. Having said that, it was obvious that, on average, the flying personnel were generally more battle-hardened and experienced than those of a normal main force bomber squadron. Shortly after my arrival I moved over to the Officers' Mess and soon found that although I had joined a smaller family' I was with excellent comrades for whom I quickly acquired considerable respect. One really did feel that one was a member of a 'crack' unit.

On the morning of 1 February 1945 I went airborne for the first time in a Mosquito with F/0 Sam Fletcher at the controls. I was to crew with Sam and regarded myself as fortunate in that respect. He was a year or two older than I was and seemed to me to be very mature as well as likeable. As I was to discover he was a most competent pilot who stayed calm in action. The only occasion I can remember him being perturbed was on a take-off from a Scottish aerodrome which had banked snow on each side of the runway. We swerved badly on take-off and the port wingtip went through the snow bank as we headed straight for a hangar, which was narrowly missed. As I was paralysed with fear his perturbation was of little account.

However, back to my first flight in a Mosquito. As I stood on the concrete I looked at the aircraft and thought what a beautiful looking aeroplane it was - so sleek and pretty com-pared with a Lancaster. Then I spotted that the NCO in charge of the ground crew was F/Sgt Jackson who lived just round the corner from me in my home town of Preston in Lancashire. Needless to say we chatted away until it was time for me to get aboard. I have to confess that my initial impression of the Mosquito as an aircraft in which to fly - as distinct from look at - was one of absolute horror as compared with aeroplanes such as Ansons, Wellingtons, Stirling's and Lancaster's in which I had flown previously.

To begin with, the engines were warming up as I climbed up the short ladder, through the trap door and into the nose of the plane. I was aghast at the proximity of the revolving propellers which seemed only a few inches away from me as I had a very healthy respect for their killing capacity. I thought to myself that there would not be much future in attempting to bale out with the 'props' so close to hand.

At this stage I should say that I stand about six feet tall and I am a shade clumsy and awkward to boot. So a clamber into the nose of a Mosquito and then, in flying kit, scramble through an opening about the size of a large rabbit hutch door into the cockpit was a thoroughly uncomfortable experience. I contemplated what chance there would be of escaping alive if the aircraft started to burn. Taking account of how difficult it would be to squeeze my frame through the opening into the nose with my parachute, dive through the trap door and dodge the propellers, I decided that the answer was - not much. Moreover, I rather fancied my skill as a navigator and I was accustomed to sitting in my curtained-off office aboard a Lancaster with a generously sized table at which to work on my charts, surrounded by my 'Gee' set, Air Position Indicator, H2S and other navigational aids. There, I could concentrate on calculating my wind speeds and course corrections almost impervious to what was going on elsewhere aboard the aircraft. I simply could not credit that, in a Mosquito, I was expected to navigate using a chart clipped to a board across my lap. I sat there and thought to myself - "My God, what have I let myself in for?" and devoutly wished to be back aboard a Lancaster!

We taxied to the end of the runway. Sam 'opened up the taps', we sped down the runway and hurtled into the sky. What a change it was compared with a Lancaster, where I scarcely ever saw light of day, to being able to view what was to be seen around me and to have the sensation of really flying, which I had only experienced previously and less comfortably during my twelve hours on Tiger Moths. After an hour or so of playing amongst the clouds we returned to base for my very first 'plot's eye view' of a high speed landing.

So I emerged from my first Mosquito flight with extremely mixed feelings. As an aeroplane in which to play at flying I thought the Mosquito was fantastic. As an aeroplane which I was to navigate in action, I was filled with foreboding.

A further half dozen familiarisation flights passed by and then I went operational with a 5 Group attack on the Mitteland canal. it was then that I discovered yet another reason for thoroughly disliking the task of navigating a Mosquito, as opposed to a Lancaster. Light. In a Lancaster one was able to flood the navigating table and instruments with light as cur-tains prevented light entering the cockpit. In a Mosquito I was expected to navigate with a small insignificant light playing on my chart. I wanted as much light as possible. Conversely, Sam, concerned about attracting night fighters, wanted as little light as possible; indeed, if it had been feasible he would have preferred me to work in the dark.

One way or another I was totally uneasy and lacking in confidence as I navigated us towards the Mitteland canal and then I had an extraordinary stroke of good fortune. At 'H-10' I announced to Sam. that by my calculations we were precisely over the target and precisely to time. Hardly had I spoken than the first batch of illuminating flares hit the sky and came cascading down around us. Never having seen them before I mistakenly supposed that they were parachutists and shouted out accordingly. To have been brought to the target with such exactitude in terms of time and position must have made Sam. think that he had acquired one of the best navigators in Bomber Command, a misapprehension which I certainly put right on a later operation when I missed the target by 40-50 miles!

Be that as it may, the next ten minutes proved to he exciting to a degree which I find difficult to put into words. The illuminating flares and searchlights made the whole area as bright as day or at least as bright as the brightest moonlight. The sky was a mass of exploding anti-aircraft shells and lazily moving streams of tracer amongst which we played a competitive game of 'who can find the target first?' Scudding above the ground at well below 1000 feet we heard one of the other markers shout "Tally Ho" and saw his marker strike the ground and burst into coloured fire. I listened as Marker Leader inspected the accuracy and gave us instructions for backing up the marker on the ground. As Sam and I dive bombed with our marker I could see the ground in almost minute detail. With our marker released and bomb doors closed we hurried off for home as fast as our two Merlins would take us. As we did so, and still hyped up from the excitement of the attack, I thought of what we had done, marvelled at the smooth organisation and knew that I would never do anything else in life which could match the excitement and elation which this form of flying offered -and I never have. It made the adrenaline run like a ten minute 'white knuckle' ride!

The operation against the Mitteland canal was repeated the following night and it proved equally exciting. Unfortunately, I was not given the opportunity to fly operationally as much as I would have liked and I had to wait until 14 March before flying again operationally. This time I was to be a Wind-Finder for the attack on the oil plant at Lutzendorf - not part of the marking team.

To be frank, I hated the job. The purpose of wind-finding was to establish an accurate measure of the wind speed and direction, at attack height in the target area, which could be fed into the bomb sight mechanism of the main force bombers. One flew to a pre-determined point close to the target, a marker was put down on the ground, and using the Mosquito's bomb-sight the navigator guided the pilot over the marker noting the precise time and air position. By repeating this operation three or four minutes later the navigator could make the required wind calculations. Three aircraft were used and by R/T the three navigators' assessments could be broadcast, with one navigator determining a mean. This would be relayed to the 'heavies' which would be closing in on the target.

My reason for detesting the work was that I simply hated having to crawl into the nose of the aircraft to crouch over and use the bombsight in such a confined space and to slide back hurriedly into the cockpit - all in full flying kit. With my height I just found it physically difficult. Fortunately I was assigned to wind-finding on only two other occasions - a repeat attack on the Lutzendorf Oil Plant on 8 April and an operation against Cham in the Sudeten Land on 17 April. Whereas, as a marker, I flew against Wurzburg, Hamburg, Molbis andKoniotau in Czechoslovakia during March and April. Additionally, I flew on the 'Gardening' operation in the River Elbe on 22 March. For me that operation was so unusual that I can still recall it clearly.

The illuminating flares were hanging over the river as our attacking Mosquitoes skimmed over the water passing by a variety of ships - at mast level - before unloading our naval mines, then disappearing into the darkness homeward bound. The scene had an eerie unreal quality about it. In the bright but artificial light one was close enough to see the faces of individual sailors. Komotau was my last operational foray before the European war ended and with the cessation of hostilities I expected to be able to hang up my navigators' kit like the proverbial cowboys' boots. But it was not to be. I was picked to crew with S/L Topper to go out to Okinawa, in a Master Bomber role, for the attacks which Tiger Force, with its Lincoln bombers - was to launch on the Japanese mainland and other Far East targets. Fancy the prospect I did not - as I detested the thought of snakes, the jungle, the heat,

Japanese treatment of air crew prisoners, etc.

Pending this overseas posting I concentrated on making hay in my leisure hours. Bill Topper was the proud owner of one of those long bonneted, open topped, quality touring cars - a Bentley I believe - which he drove over to his home in the Manchester area. So I was always good for a lift most of the way home. It was on one of these home visits that the news broke of the dropping of the atomic bomb on Hiroshima. I had travelled from Preston to Manchester early in the morning and was waiting for Bill Topper to pick me up when I heard of the new weapon being used for the first time. It was quite obvious that no nation could sustain attacks of that kind and that the war with Japan must rapidly reach its end in some way or another. So it was, my fighting war, thankfully, had come to an end; indeed by the end of July I had ceased flying. I ask myself what are my most outstanding memories of my time with 627 Squadron as I look back after more than forty five years. Without a doubt THE memory is the sheer physical thrill of being a member of an operational target marking team, flying below the illuminating flares hunting for the aiming point with desperately little time to spare - see-ing the gun-fire flashing past - dive bombing the target - and finally rushing off into the night. A package of thrills which few people ever experience in an entire life-time.

But I do have other memories, especially of people who were such good friends and with whom I had so many good - and wild - times when we were not flying. So wild that as many of them will still be alive and now be sedate, respectable, grandfathers that it is probably wise not to elaborate on that theme or name names.

I also remember how 'cool' some of these individuals were. For instance, I'm not likely to forget flying with F/0 Endean in a 'clapped out' Lancaster which we were using for H2S MWI trials when he calmly proposed to loop the plane. Had he not been persuaded, with not a little difficulty, to refrain, I am sure that the wings would have dropped off. Nor S/L Topper flying under cloud and descending bombs to establish the accuracy of a blind bombing attack. Nor the coolness of F/L Armstrong when, on a sight seeing trip after the war had ended, we 'lost' an engine over the Rhine and had to make an emergency landing at Melsbroek, near Brussels.

All in all those few months which I spent, so long ago, with 627 Squadron were among the most significant - and formative - of my life.

Informal Dress.
F/L Armstrong and F/O Burke in the summer of 1945.

Photograph: Bill Burke Collection.

EINE KLEINE NACHT ARBEIT (All in a nights work)
By Phil George

The question 'What did you do in the war Daddy?' conjures up an image of golden haired innocence gazing wonderingly - even admiringly - at the grey haired (hopefully) wrinkled (certainly) face of its parent. After gazing thoughtfully into the distance for a suitable period, designed to give the impression of concentrated thought, in fact trying to remember which war, he replies, 'I surrendered dear.'

The old man imagines this is a wonderful opportunity to fascinate his offspring with hair-raising accounts of airborne adventure. Unfortunately, before he can marshal his memories the golden wonder is already bashing away on the keys of his laptop. I am that old man and, undeterred by the child's reluctance to be fascinated, I propose to subject you to what she missed - albeit in small doses.

Phil George. Third from left

After the usual induction into military thinking, procedures, discipline, etc. our crew found themselves posted to 9 Squadron at Bardney in late November 1943. At that time the so-called 'Battle of Berlin' was gaining momentum and the 'chop-rate' was causing some concern; thankfully a statistic unknown to most of us.

In those days it was customary for the pilot of a 'sprog' crew to go on a 'second dicky' operating as second pilot, with an experienced crew so that when he took his own crew on his first sortie he had some idea of what was going on when people started shooting at you and, better still, what to do about it. The instinctive and rational action, to turn round and go home, was discouraged. Whether the ploy was generally successful I do not know, but suffice it to say, it did not work in our case because after going all the way to Berlin and back, the crew with whom our pilot had flown crashed near Louth and most of them were killed. Since this event occurred within eighteen hours of our arrival at Bardney it rather knocked the stuffing out of us since we were still trying to find our way around the depressing sites, damp Nissen huts and mud of an unfamiliar locality in the semi-darkness of a wet November.

A rather poignant memory at this juncture - another member of our crew, an Australian and I took it upon ourselves to travel down to Cheltenham where our skipper's mother lived and did our best to comfort her. Retrospectively, I recognise that although perhaps our motivation was meritorious both of us at twenty years of age and with virtually no experience of life, were assuming a lot. All I recall of this incident was a reception far more worthy than the circumstances warranted.

Like the proverbial headless chicken we circled the farmyard until the military equivalent of the National Lottery ejected a ball annotated with the name Wing Commander E.K. Piercy. He was a regular officer who had returned from operating twin-engine aircraft in the Middle East and now had to convert to 'fours' before becoming involved in the European theatre. Additionally, he had to assimilate assorted aviators of whose competence, temperament and current rather depressed state, he had no knowledge; our feelings, in reverse, were probably not dissimilar. He was to become our replacement pilot and eventually Commanding Officer of 106 Squadron.

Our crew, complete once again, duly returned to 1661 Heavy Conversion Unit at Winthorpe to repeat the course we had completed on Lancaster's, the previous autumn. This time around our new pilot had to master the mighty Stirling because the 'Lancs.' had been withdrawn from these units to replace the losses being suffered by the operational squadrons. This, of course, necessitated a short course at No 5 Lancaster Finishing School at RAF Syerston to convert from Stirling's to Lancaster's.

The return to the Newark area produced some complications in the love life of one or two of the crew who had moved to pastures new. It is also worth noting that, because of the large numbers of aircrew operating in the area, some pastures were very thinly sown with the result that competition to reap where one had sown was fierce indeed.

However, those minor hiccups having been overcome, the arrival of a new CO at RAF Metheringham in mid-March 1944 was duly recorded in Air Ministry records and noted with some curiosity at the airfield itself.

EINE KLEINE SCHRECHT (A little night fright)

Wing Commander 'Ronnie' Baxter, who was our skipper's immediate predecessor, had been a very popular and effective CO of 106 Squadron, a circumstance of which Wg Cdr Piercy must surely have been well aware and accordingly the latter would have wished to establish himself as a worthy successor. Therefore, when we launched ourselves into the night sky at 1920 hours on 24th March 1944, we were not only operational for the first time, but we were going to be over Berlin first or bust! This was not to be; the German capital was to be spared the attentions of at least one *terror flieger* that night.

The cloud base was about 800 feet, which meant that shortly after take-off we would have been climbing blind most if not all the way to our briefed altitude. Quite what happened at the front end I don't know, but suffice it to say that Piercy suddenly found himself denied the essential information provided by the instrument flying panel. This consisted of, amongst other items that provided by the airspeed indicator, the altimeter and the artificial horizon. The loss of any one of these instruments would have made flying in cloud and staying in the air difficult, the loss of them all precluded any further progress whatsoever. In these circumstances Piercy announced that we would have to abort the trip and since we all wanted to stay in the air there was no dissension in the ranks, but we were, in what was referred to in those days as a hairy situation.

We had a full fuel load, a bomb load consisting of primarily incendiaries and one 4,000lb bomb, a 'cookie', which, because of its explosive properties, could not safely be dropped below an altitude of 4,000ft without destroying the aircraft that had dropped it. Since we could not climb above 800ft this device became something of an embarrassment.

I was immediately called upon to demonstrate my navigational skills when Piercy demanded a course for the coast, in a somewhat peremptory tone I thought. However, having been born in Newark and visited both 'Skeggie' and Sutton-in-Sea in childhood and remembering that they lay to the east of Metheringham, I duly responded and off we went.

After some minutes bumping along at 600ft the skipper again issued an order, to Doug Morton, our Australian Bomb Aimer, 'jettison the incendiaries when safe to do so' and further announced that he was 'preparing to jettison fuel shortly'.

In passing it is worth noting that as the Squadron CO, he always used our surnames or our crew category when addressing any member of the crew, in the circumstances in which we found ourselves this did not seem to matter. But, retrospectively, I feel that we lacked the camaraderie that other crews, which had less exalted pilots, enjoyed.

The incendiaries were duly dropped, but on reaching Lincolnshire they immediately ignited, our rear gunner Stan Goodman excitedly reported that we were leaving a long trail of fires across the Fens. (I'm surprised that a German raider didn't drop his bombs thinking it was a flare path. Editor) I won't attempt to replicate the language with which he revealed his excitement, nor those words with which Piercy received the report. After this little drama the fuel dumping proceeded without incident perhaps because Piercy was so impressed with the skills his crew were demonstrating, that a little time must have elapsed between us leaving the fires behind and our spraying high octane fuel over the countryside.

Now, we were faced with the problem of landing back at Metheringham with the 4,000lb device, which still hung threateningly in the bomb bay. We all recognised that this was an highly hazardous procedure and would require the demonstration of an highly skilled and delicate touch down in order to avoid any jerk or sudden movement, dislodging the bomb and thus necessitating the appointment of a new CO and crew.

Although strict R/T silence was normally mandatory throughout an operation from leaving dispersal to return, in the circumstances Piercy advised the control tower of our situation and we did a few circuits of the airfield while the tower was evacuated and give sufficient time to alert all personnel likely to be effected, to take cover in case of a problem.

Whatever the reaction of the 'authorities' to the events of that night Piercy certainly earned the admiration and respect of everyone- especially ourselves - for the quality of his airmanship, in putting us all back on the ground almost without the ground itself knowing we had landed.

No one could deny that on our first operation we must have created quite an impression - if not on the runway itself - then certainly in the minds of the rest of the personnel of 106.

I LEARNED ABOUT FLYING FROM THAT

By John Tulk

As a member of the Aircrew Association, I am among a minority. All my flying was post World War 2. I can tell no tales of danger or heroism in face of the enemy, as so many of the other stories in this book describe. Any danger I faced was caused by my own incompetence, stupidity, or carelessness, so my story is about that.

Other members of that post-war minority group may realise that I have taken my title from a flight-safety magazine that was published regularly throughout the 1950s and 60s (and possibly later). Aircrew were able to submit anonymous articles describing irregular acts of flying, in the belief that other aircrew might learn from their mistakes.

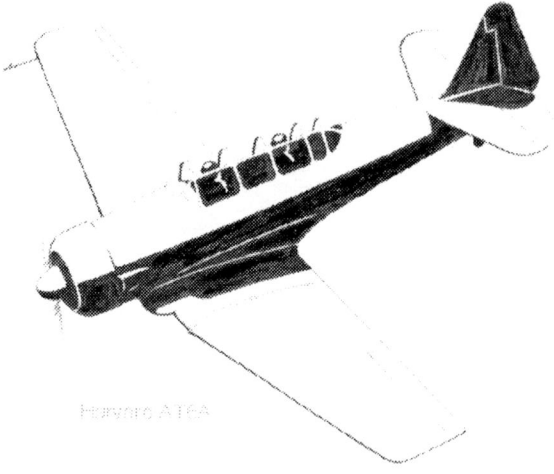

The incident I describe happened in 1961. At the time I was a member of RAF Handling Squadron, the unit responsible for preparing and maintaining the handling, drills, and emergencies sections of Pilot's Notes for all aircraft in service with the RAF, the Royal Navy, the Army, and for some Commonwealth air forces. Six pilots, a flight commander and C.O. had responsibility for the books for one hundred and fourteen types of aircraft. My main aircraft were all the V-bombers (Valiant, Vulcan's, and Victor's) but if I mention that among my list of other aircraft were the Beaufighter and Mosquito it will be obvious by that time there was little work to be done on the Pilot's Notes for them.

I was sitting in my office at Boscombe Down and engaged in writing the first draft of Pilot's Notes for the Victor B Mk2, when the telephone rang. "John. Can you fly a Harvard?" asked the voice on the other end. It took me a moment to realise that it was the Superintendent of Flying who was asking me. What an unexpected question and especially from him. He didn't usually call an ordinary squadron pilot directly like that. Of course I could fly a Harvard. I had trained on Harvard's and had instructed on them, accumulating some hundreds of hours in the process. It had been about seven years since I had last flown one but obviously I said that I could.

"Oh Good" came his response. "We've got an Argosy over the (Salisbury) Plain, waiting to drop a tank, and a photographer sitting in the Harvard waiting to film it, but the pilot's just fallen and hurt himself. It's urgent that we complete this trial today, and I'd go myself but I've got a visitor coming soon. So can you take it? The plane's all ready."

Obviously I couldn't refuse such a request, especially from him. So off I went to grab my flying kit. At that time I was used to flying a variety of aircraft. In the few months before I had flown various marks of Victor and Vulcan plus Valiant, Canberra, Argosy, Meteor, Hunter, Javelin, Jet Provost, Chipmunk, and Anson. Some of these I was only vaguely familiar with so usually I had a look at their Pilots' Notes before flying them. Naturally I wanted to check the notes for a Harvard, having not flown one for so long, but couldn't find them in the rack where they should have been. I even checked the adjacent slots, just in case they had been filed wrongly, but still no luck. Anyway, off I went, feeling sure it would all come back to me

The ground crew had already started the engine for me and told me that the parachute was in the seat ready for me to fasten it on. There, sitting in the rear cockpit and holding up his left hand to show me his watch as he tapped it meaningfully was the civilian photographer, obviously anxious to be on the way to do his job as quickly as possible. I did my best to meet his wishes, casting my eyes around the cockpit to re-familiarise myself and check that all was OK as I strapped myself in. As soon as I plugged into the intercom he told me that we had only a few minutes in which to get to the dropping zone so, after another quick check around I waved away the chocks and moved out of the dispersal.

Boscombe Down had a 4000 yard runway and as I entered the perimeter track we were almost level with the upwind end of it. It would take a long time to taxi to the other end and I could see three other aircraft taxiing out ahead of me to the take-off point. I called the tower and asked for permission to make an expedited short take-off by joining the runway at the nearest entry point, explaining the need for my urgency. That would give me a take-off run of just a few hundred yards but quite sufficient for a little plane like a Harvard. With permission granted I did my pre-take-off checks as I taxied towards the runway and then swung onto it, opening the throttle steadily as I lined myself up.

Now we were off, or so I thought. The aircraft accelerated and the tail came up rather more quickly than I had expected. It also started to swing left across the quite wide runway and I had to apply much more pressure with my right foot than I ever remembered being necessary, even though I knew the Harvard had a reputation for swinging. Having corrected the swing I suddenly realised that we were now approaching the end of the runway rather quickly and the aircraft was showing no signs of lifting off. Rather the opposite. I was having to pull back on the stick to prevent the nose from going further down, even though we were still on the ground. Admittedly the last time I had flown this type of plane I had flown it from the rear cockpit, where the view forwards is not all that good, but it still seemed very strange to me now and I was worried as well as puzzled. But we had to get airborne quickly for I could see the end of the runway getting rapidly nearer. It took me all my strength to get that aircraft up off the runway and then hold the nose up to climb away. As I struggled with it I heard the chap behind me mutter "Crikey! That was a bit close. "

It was too. We were only just clearing the poles of the runway approach lights. Obviously there was something wrong with the aircraft trim for now I was having to use both hands on the stick to keep the nose up and still having to apply a lot of right rudder. I was about to explain to him the trouble I was having when I suddenly realised why. On the Harvard there are two metal wheels, approximately dinner-plate sized, positioned vertically fore and aft and side by side close to the pilot's left foot. Those wheels are used to adjust the settings of the trim tabs on the aircraft elevators and rudder. The settings for take-off are neutral trim for the elevators and fully right trim for the rudder, with notches and bumps on the wheels edges for the pilot to feel how he has set them without having to peer down. In my hurry to get airborne I must have set the trim wrongly. I had set fully nose-down trim on the elevator and neutral trim on the rudder! No wonder I had had trouble both with keeping straight and with lifting the aircraft off the runway to climb away. As I hastened to correct my stupid mistake I remembered a phrase written by a fellow instructor to describe the flying of one of his pupils.

"Bloggs is a strong fellow and regularly displays his strength when in the air!"

I had just had to display my strength like that, because of my own sheer stupidity. I was in a hurry but, being well out of practice at flying this particular type of aircraft, I should have stopped and spent just a few extra moments doing my checks properly before taking off. I'd been overconfident and stupid. Because of that I had come close to killing myself as well as the trusting and innocent photographer sitting in the cockpit behind me.

My arms and legs felt quite limp as I climbed away from the airfield, changed the radio channel and contacted the pilot of the Argosy to arrange our rendezvous. It is an amazing sight to see at close quarters as first the drogue and then the pilot chute appear from the rear doors of a big aircraft, then slowly pull out a full-sized tank. It swung down as it fell from the Argosy and I wheeled down to follow it as the main parachutes (five of them I think) slowly deployed. The photographer had his hatch open so he could film everything as we watched the tank gradually stop swinging and descend steadily to the field below. Having seen it land he asked me to make a low-level run across the field past the tank and then we were on our way back to base.

Never have I been so glad to get an aircraft back onto the ground. The strange thing was that, once on the approach I forgot my tenseness which had been present throughout the flight when I kept thinking about how close I had come to pranging. Now suddenly it all felt familiar to me again and I had no trouble in setting the aircraft down with a good three-point landing. As we taxied in the photographer, who I was to learn was extremely experienced and probably had more hours flying in Harvard's than I had, actually thanked me for a very comfortable flight and then asked me if I would be able to take him on another sortie the next day. Not surprisingly, I did not tell him how close I had come to killing us both. But I'd learned a heck of a lot about flying.

BECHERS BROOK

By Michael W. Cross

"Ah ! Cross I see you have just come back from 73 Squadron in Malta. Now let me see what posting we can offer you. - Fancy flying Sabres? The F86 Sabre was an American super- sonic jet fighter and as far as I knew none were in service with the Royal Air Force. "Too right" I replied The Officer went on to say that there was a job just starting, bringing Sabres back from Canada, called "Operation Bechers Brook"

Operation "Bechers Brook" is probably one of the least well known but probably one of the most interesting operations ever undertaken by the R.A.F. in peacetime. During `53 it involved the safe ferrying of four hundred Sabre jet fighters from Montreal Canada to England. Over three thousand one hundred miles of almost uninhabited land, desolate ice and sea that could kill within minutes anyone forced down into it.. The ground crews, many National Servicemen, worked often in sub-zero conditions servicing and refueling aircraft;

The idea of the Operation was born in the spring of `52 when with the cold war shivering the confidence of the Western Defense Chiefs, a Mutual Aid Scheme was arranged by which Britain was allocated four hundred of the latest design American planes to be manufactured under license in Canada. The R.A.F. was badly in need of fighter aircraft capable of super-sonic speed that could more than match any that the Russians could put up.

The route from St.Hubert near Montreal lay across Labrador to Goose Bay where the first landing was made. Then on to Bluie West One in Greenland. Here there was only one runway marked out by stained lines in the snow and the approach had to be made by flying up a narrow fjord flanked by mountains. As if that was not enough at the end of the runway was a glacier. The next flight was to Keflavic in Iceland and then on to Kinloss in Scotland. From there the aircraft were delivered to the Maintenance Unit at Kemble.

The flying suits were rubber immersion suits and adequate survival equipment was provided in the Sabre. On the sea routes a weather ship would be situated half way and would be over flown.

A convoy would be made up of sections of four aircraft which would take off separated by five minute intervals. On my third crossing I was flying as No2 to the C.O. and at 35,00ft. just passed the point of no return between Goose Bay and Bluie West One I felt my aileron controls freeze up and I was without any aileron control. The C.O. told me I could bale out over the weather ship if I wished but anyway break off from the formation. From way out I could see Greenland and I elected to stay with it. I let down slowly hoping the controls would unfreeze and maintained direction with the rudder. I was soon able to pick up the runway and line up without turning. All went well until I was over the mountains at a low level when turbulence became a problem, but rudder control overcame this--just. A safe landing was made and the controls unfroze when the Flt, Sgt got in to check. I got cheered up in the Mess later when an American pilot said "Gee Mac I would have been straight over the side" The controls were dried out but half way to Iceland - froze again. This time the let down was through cloud. A very gentle let down and left turn using rudder only to line up with the runway and all was well . This time when the Flt. Sgt got in to check they were still frozen.

When modified to R.A.F. standard the Sabres went to stations in Germany and were eventually replaced by the Hunter.

"HE HAD TO GO AND PRANG 'ER IN THE HANGER"

He had to go and prang 'er in the hanger.
Forgetting all his teachers good advice.
He made a landing slap against the windsock.
And sat admidst the wreckage in a trice.
The duty pilot phoned up his dispersal.
His Flight Commander took a gloomy view.
And his C.O. who was watching from the window.
Said "Oh what a clottish thing to do."
Next day he went to see the fierce Group Captain.
Who said "It is too big a job for me.
A fragrant piece of carelessness like this, Sir.
Must come at once before the A.O.C.
For you had to go and prang her in the hanger.
And though it is the first of your mishaps.
Let me tell you even Wing Commanders Flying.
Are not allowed to land without their flaps".
Next day the much be-ribboned Air Vice Marshal.
Received him with a cold and glassy stare.
And said "Although to pilots I am partial.
To let the matter rest I do not dare".
"Why did he have to prang it in the hanger."

He whispered to his stooge upon the right.
"The Chief will have to see the boy tomorrow.
I'll contact him at Claridges tonight".
The C .in C.. was yawning when he entered.
And didn't seem to know why he had come.
But when he heard he'd pranged a brand new Spitfire.
He banged his desk so hard he hurt his thumb.
"So you have to go and prang her in the hanger.
You've put up an unprecedented black.
The Air Council are meeting in the morning.
If I didn't send you there I'd get the sack."
But the Air Council referred the cowering culprit.
To His Majesty himself to judge the case.
For they said that being merely Air Chief Marshals.
They really couldn't cope with such disgrace.
The Daily Mirror featured it in headlines.
"Spitfire pilot sent before the King".
The Brains Trust soon decided on the wireless
If this was treason he would have to swing.
He had to go and prang her in the hanger.
People said from Chelsea to the Strand.
Remember Dear what happened in Malaya.
Why can't they have a unified command.
His Majesty was smiling when he entered.
And offered him a Turkish cigarette.
And said "I've had to deal with some strange cases.
But this is quite the most perplexing yet.
I'm told you had to go and prang her in the hanger.
It reminds me of myself when as a boy,
They let me go and fly a brand new Sopwith.

Which then was quite the latest kind of toy.
But I had to go and prang her in the hanger.
And worked myself into a fearful stew.
But the Flight Commander said "You needn't worry,
Its really quite the normal thing to do".
"And now that you have no stripes worth the tearing.
You're free, my fighter pilot, you can go.
But this is my advice - Do not go and do it twice.
Once is quite enough to prang her in the hanger".

GLOSSARY

AAEE	Aircraft and Armament Experimental Est.
A/C	Aircraft or Aircrew
Ack Ack or AA	Anti aircraft fire
ACRC	Aircrew Receiving Centre
AFC	Air Force Cross
AFM	Air Force Medal
AM	Air Ministry or Air Marshal
APU	Auxiliary power unit
ASI	Air speed indicator
ASP	Air servicing pan
ATA	Actual time of arrival or Air Transport. Aux.
AVM	Air Vice Marshal
Bandit or Bogy	Enemy Aircraft
BAT	Beam Approach Training
B/A	Bomb Aimer
B & G	Bombing & Gunnery
BFP	Blind flying panel
BFTS	British Flying Training School
Block buster	Very heavy bomb
C	Corporal
CC	Coastal Command
CFI	Chief Flying Instructor
Chaff	Aluminium strip to foil radar
CU	Conversion Unit
Darky	Night emergency RT.
D/F	Direction Finding
DFC	Distinguished Flying Cross

DFM	Distinguished Flying Medal
Driver	Pilot
DR	Dead reckoning
EFTS	Elementary Flying Training School
ETA	Estimated time of arrival
ETPS	Empire Test Pilots School
FIDO	Fog intensive dispersal organisation
F/C	Flight Commander
F/L	Flight Lieutenant
F/O	Flying Officer
F/ENG	Flight Engineer
F/G	Front Gunner
Flak	Anti aircraft fire
F/S	Flight Sergeant
FREYA	German radar aerial
GATU	Ground Attack Training Unit
G/C	Group Captain
GEE	Radar position fixer
George	Automatic pilot
Grand Slam	22,000 lb. bomb
HCU	Heavy Conversion Unit
H2S	Radar ground picture
Hit the Silk	Parachute Down
IFF	Identification friend or foe
ITW	Initial Training Wing
LAC	Leading Aircraftsman
LFS	Lancaster Finishing School
M.C	Master of Ceremonies or Military Cross
MU	Maintenance Unit
MUG	Mid upper gunner

NAV	Navigator
OBOE	Radio beam navigation system
O/C	Officer Commanding
OTU	Operational Training Unit
PACTC	Preliminary A/C Training Course
PF	Path Finders
PRU	Photo Reconnaissance Unit
RDF	Radio direction finding
RG	Rear Gunner
RECCE	Reconnaissance
R/T	Radio transmissions
SFTS	Service Flying Training School
S/L	Squadron Leader
SOE	Special Operations Executive
Tallboy	12,000 lb. earthquake bomb
U/S	Unserviceable
USAAC	United States Army Air Corps
UT	Under training
Very Light	Recognition firework signal
White Caps	Surf on the Water
W/C	Wing Commander
W/OP	Wireless Operator
W/T	Wireless telegraphy
Window	Aluminium strip to foil radar
Z (Hours)	Greenwich Mean Time

THE GREMLINS

When you're seven miles up in the heavens
And that's a hell of a lonely spot
And its 50 degrees below zero
Which isn't exactly hot
When you're frozen blue like your Spitfire
And scared a Mosquito pink
When you're thousands of miles from nowhere
And there's nothing below but the drink
It`s then you will see the Gremlins
Green and gamboge and gold
Male and female and neuter
Gremlins both young and old

White ones will wiggle your wing tips
Male ones will muddle your maps
Green ones will guzzle your glycol
Females will flutter your flaps
Pink ones will pitch on your perspex
And dance pirouettes on your prop
There's one spherical middle aged gremlin
Who spins on your stick like a top
They'll freeze up your camera shutter
They'll bite through your aileron wires
They'll cause your whole tail to flutter
They'll insert toasting forks in your tyres

This is the song of the Gremlins as sung by the P.R.U.
Pretty ruddy unlikely to many but fact none the less to the few.